MAINTAINING *the* *Marriage* COVENANT

Mariana Vanstipelen

Edited and Published by Shekinah Editions

Maintaining The Marriage Covenant
© 2026 By Shekinah Editions

A publication of the Shekinah Editions.
Scriptures are mainly quoted from the KJV and NKJV of The Bible.

Design and distribution by Bublish

ISBN: 979-8-89989-120-5

Contents

Foreword

Marriage is one of the most sacred institutions God created. It is not merely a social contract or a legal agreement; it is a *Divine Covenant* designed to reflect the love between Christ and His Church. Yet in today's world, many couples struggle to experience the joy, peace, and purpose that God intended for their union. Too often, what was meant to be "a little bit of heaven on earth" becomes a battlefield of misunderstandings, unmet expectations, and spiritual dryness.

That is why this book, *Maintaining The Marriage Covenant*, is both timely and necessary.

In these pages, the author speaks not only from biblical insight but also from heartfelt experience. This book does not shy away from the realities of marriage, the highs and the lows. Instead, it offers hope, healing, and holy perspective. It reminds couples that a good marriage doesn't just happen; it is built daily on faith, prayer, communication, and mutual sacrifice.

This book brings a fresh light and deeper revelation for couples seeking more than just survival in marriage. It points the way to revival. Whether you are newly married, have been walking together for decades, or are preparing for marriage, this book will bless you with truth, tools, and spiritual encouragement.

As you read, may your heart be stirred to pursue not just a good marriage, but a *covenant* one, where love flows freely, peace reigns, and God is glorified. Let this book be your guide as you build a good home through a marriage rooted in Christ.

J.R.F. Vanstipelen

Preface

Marriage is not merely a social institution or a legal agreement; it is a sacred covenant established by God. From the beginning, God designed marriage to reflect His own faithful, unchanging love. When a man and a woman enter into marriage, they not only make promises to one another, but they stand before God and invite Him to be the center of their covenant.

Yet, in our generation, the marriage covenant is under great pressure. Many couples begin their journey with love and hope, but along the way, they face challenges such as unmet expectations, communication breakdown, financial strain, spiritual neglect, and external influences. These pressures, if not addressed with wisdom and prayer, can slowly weaken what God intended to be strong and enduring.

This book was written out of a deep pastoral burden and love for families. Over the years, I have walked with couples through seasons of joy and seasons of pain, and I have seen that marriages thrive not by chance, but by intentional commitment to God's principles. A strong marriage is maintained when both spouses choose covenant over convenience, forgiveness over offense, and obedience to God over personal desire.

Maintaining the marriage covenant requires more than emotions; it requires faith, humility, prayer, and daily surrender to God. When Christ remains at the center, marriage becomes a place of growth, healing, companionship, and spiritual strength. As Ecclesiastes 4:12 reminds us, "A threefold cord is not quickly broken."

It is my prayer that this book will serve as a guide, an encouragement, and a spiritual tool for couples who desire to honor God in their marriage. Whether you are newly married, walking through challenges, or seeking to strengthen an already healthy union, may these pages lead you back to God's original design and renew your commitment to the sacred covenant.

May the Lord strengthen your marriage, restore hope, and unite you in a threefold cord with Him at the center.

In Christ's love,
Pastor Mariana Vanstipelen

Acknowledgments

Writing a book, especially one as close to the heart as this, is never a solitary journey. I am deeply grateful to the many whose support, love, prayers, and encouragement made this book possible.

First and foremost, I thank **God Almighty**, the Author of love and the Designer of marriage. Without His wisdom, grace, and presence, this book would have no meaning. The Holy Spirit inspires every page of this book. All Glory belongs to God.

To my beloved husband *J.R.F. Vanstipelen*, thank you for walking this journey with me. Your love, patience, and class have been a living testimony of God's design for marriage.

To our children Eunice and Joshua, thank you for your understanding during the long hours of writing, praying, and reflecting. Your support means more than words can express.

A heartfelt thank you to our church family and ministry team, who continually encourage and strengthen us. Your prayers and feedback have shaped this work in powerful ways. Special thanks to the couples and individuals who shared their testimonies and allowed their stories to be part of this message.

To my editor, proofreaders, and publishing team, thank you for your professionalism and commitment to excellence. Your work helped bring this vision to life with clarity and impact.

Finally, to every reader, thank you for opening your heart to this message. May this book lead you into deeper intimacy with God and with your spouse. May your home be filled with joy, peace, and the glory of the Lord.

With love and gratitude,
Mariana Vanstipelen

Introduction

MARRIAGE IS GOD'S DESIGN

God's design for marriage was intentional, sacred, and full of purpose. He envisioned it as a divine alliance between a man and a woman, where two hearts and lives are joined together in love, mutual respect, and unity, reflecting His own nature. Marriage was created to be beautiful: a sanctuary of intimacy, joy, and companionship; a purposeful union that fulfills His plans and glorifies His name; and a powerful force for good that shapes families, blesses communities, and leaves a lasting legacy for generations to come.

Yet in our modern world, many people have lost sight of that vision. Marriage has become misunderstood, devalued, or even feared. Some see it as outdated, others see it as too difficult, and many have entered it without a clear understanding of what God truly intended. As a result, homes that should be filled with laughter and love are instead marked by silence, strife, and sorrow.

But it doesn't have to be that way.

This book is a call to return to God's original design, a call to rediscover marriage as a sacred covenant, not just a social contract. It's a journey into understanding how a good marriage can be a *heavenly experience*, even in an imperfect world. A relationship where grace flows, forgiveness is constant, and both husband and wife pursue God together.

A Divine Blueprint

In Genesis 2:18, God said, *"It is not good that the man should be alone; I will make him a helper comparable to him."* And so, He created a woman, not as an afterthought, but as a vital partner in God's divine plan. Marriage was the first human relationship God ever established. It came before the Church, before the government, before any human institution. That tells us something: marriage is not man's idea; it's God's.

The union between a man and a woman is a powerful picture of the union between Christ and His Bride: the Church. (Ephesians 5:22–33). When we live according to His pattern, loving, submitting, forgiving, and serving each other, we step into something sacred and supernatural.

Why Marriages Struggle

So why do many marriages struggle with this reality?

One reason is misplaced expectations. Many couples go into marriage thinking their spouse will complete them, make them happy all the time, or fix their insecurities. But marriage was never meant to take the place of God in our lives. When we place our ultimate expectations in God, He faithfully supplies what no human can.

Another reason is spiritual neglect. When couples stop praying together, stop reading the Word, and stop seeking God's will for their home, the foundation begins to crack. The enemy knows the power of a united praying couple, and he does everything possible to divide and distract them.

There is also the matter of *ignorance.* Many people simply don't know what God says about marriage. They've never been taught how to resolve conflict, communicate with love, or build intimacy in a Godly way. They repeat what they saw growing up or what the world portrays, but that's often far from biblical truth.

Hope for Every Marriage

The good news is this: no matter where your marriage stands today, whether it's thriving, surviving, or struggling, *there is hope*. With God, nothing is too broken to be restored. He is the One who turns water into wine (John 2:1–11), and He can turn bitterness into sweetness, strife into peace, and coldness into compassion.

This book is not just theory. It is filled with biblical principles, practical tools, and spiritual encouragement to help you walk in the reality of a *good and Godly marriage*. A marriage where heaven is not just a far-away promise, but a present experience.

You will discover how to:

- Build your marriage on Christ as your solid foundation.

- Communicate with love, respect, and understanding.

- Pray together and grow spiritually as a couple.

- Handle conflicts with wisdom and grace.

- Keep your love fresh, joyful, and lasting.

- Raise Godly children in a unified home.

- And reflect God's glory through your relationship.

Let Heaven Begin at Home

We often pray, *"Let Your will be done on earth as it is in Heaven."* What if that began in your marriage? What if your home could be a sanctuary of peace, a garden of joy, a training ground for Godliness, and a testimony to the world of God's love?

That is what this book is about. It's an invitation to experience marriage the way God intended it: full of purpose, power, and divine presence.

As you read, I encourage you to pray. Invite the Holy Spirit to speak to you through every chapter. Whether you are reading this alone or with your spouse, open your heart and let God do a new work in your home.

Marriage can be a taste of heaven on earth if you allow God to be the center of it.

Let the journey begin.

PART I

Foundations of a Godly Marriage

CHAPTER 1

God's Original Design for Marriage

"And the Lord God said, 'It is not good that man should be alone; I will make him a helper comparable to him.'"

Marriage was not man's idea; it was God's. In the very beginning, before the fall of man, before sin entered the world, and even before there was a government, there was marriage. This reveals the sacredness and centrality of marriage in God's Divine plan for humanity. It is not just a social contract or legal agreement; it is a holy covenant ordained by the Creator of heaven and earth.

1. Marriage is God's Initiative

Genesis 2:18 says, *"And the Lord God said, 'It is not good that man should be alone; I will make him a helper comparable to him.'"* This is the first time in Scripture that God declares something "not good." Up until this point, all of creation was called "good" or "very good." But Adam's aloneness was not good; not because he was incomplete or defective, but because God designed humanity for relationship, for fellowship, and for partnership.

God did not bring Eve from the dust, as He did with Adam. Instead, He took a rib from Adam's side and formed the woman. This divine act signifies unity, intimacy, and equality. She was not taken from his head to rule over him, nor from his feet to be trampled by him, but from his side to walk with him, from under his arm to be protected, and near his heart to be loved.

2. Marriage Reflects God's Nature and Image

Genesis 1:27–28 says, *"So God created man in His own image; in the image of God He created him; male and female He created them. Then God blessed them, and God said to them, 'Be fruitful and multiply.'"*

God's image is best reflected when both male and female come together in unity. In marriage, we reflect the relational nature of God, the unity and love that exists within the Trinity: Father, Son, and Holy Spirit. This is not simply about reproduction; it's about reflecting God's glory through love, trust, sacrifice, and faithfulness.

The Apostle Paul later confirms this in Ephesians 5:31–32, where he explains that the union between husband and wife is a mystery that points to Christ and the Church. This shows that marriage is not just about companionship, it is about purpose and spiritual symbolism.

3. God Designed Marriage for Companionship and Purpose

When God said He would make a "helper suitable for him," the Hebrew word used is *ezer kenegdo;* a word that denotes strength and support, not weakness or inferiority. In fact, the word ezer is also used to describe God Himself as a helper (Psalm 33:20). Eve was created as a powerful, suitable partner for Adam, not a servant but a co-laborer. Together, the man and woman were to:

- Enjoy fellowship with God

- Cultivate and guard the Garden

- Multiply and fill the earth

- Rule and steward creation: dominion.

This shows us that marriage is not merely about physical intimacy or social security; it is about *Divine assignment.* God's design for marriage involves spiritual, emotional, and practical unity to fulfill His mandate on the earth.

4. Marriage Is a Covenant, Not a Contract

Unlike a contract, which is based on mutual benefit and can be broken when one party fails, a *covenant* is based on a promise before God and involves deep, personal commitment. In Malachi 2:14, God calls marriage a *covenant*, and He rebukes those who deal treacherously with the spouse of their youth.

This covenant is not just horizontal (between husband and wife) but vertical (with God as the third cord). That's why Ecclesiastes 4:12 says, *"A cord of three strands is not easily broken."* When God is truly the center of your marriage, that union becomes strong, resilient, and fruitful.

5. Marriage Requires Leaving, Cleaving, and Becoming One

Genesis 2:24 says, *"Therefore a man shall leave his father and mother and be joined to his wife, and they shall **become** one flesh."* This verse gives us the foundational steps of a Godly marriage:

Leaving: Emotionally and practically leaving the parental home and becoming independent. This doesn't mean dishonoring parents but establishing a new priority and loyalty in marriage.

Cleaving: Clinging to each other in commitment. The Hebrew term means to be glued or bonded. Marriage requires intentional bonding spiritually, emotionally, physically, and even financially.

Becoming One: This refers to deep unity, not just sexual union, but also heart, purpose, and life journey. "One flesh" means working as a team, praying together, dreaming together, forgiving quickly, and carrying each other's burdens.

6. The Fall Distorted God's Design, But Grace Restores It

After Adam and Eve sinned, the harmony in their relationship was disrupted. Blame and fear entered the marriage. This shows us that sin always tries to destroy what God has joined together.

But in Christ, we are given the power to restore what was broken. Jesus came to bring us back to God's original design, not just in our personal lives but also in our marriages. Through forgiveness, humility, and the help of the Holy Spirit, couples can experience the joy, peace, and unity that God intended from the beginning.

A Return to the Blueprint

To have a marriage that reflects heaven on earth, we must return to *God's original blueprint*. This means making Christ the foundation, honoring God's Word, and walking in love daily. A good marriage is not automatic; it must be cultivated with prayer, sacrifice, grace, and mutual honor.

When we follow God's original design, marriage becomes more than just a partnership; it becomes a holy sanctuary where God's presence dwells, where children are nurtured in righteousness, and where both husband and wife grow into their divine destinies. Truly, such a marriage is a taste of heaven on earth.

CHAPTER 2

The Covenant, Not a Contract

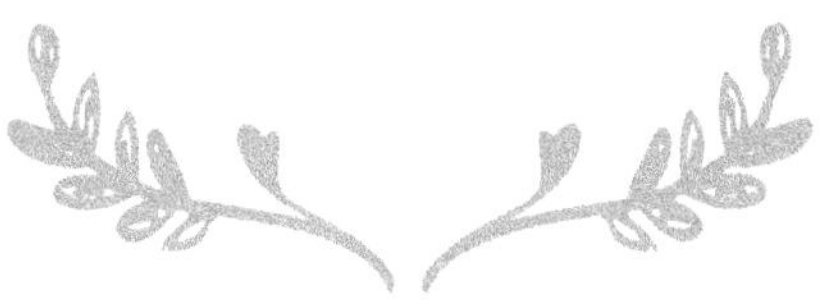

"Yet she is your companion and your wife by covenant." Malachi 2:14

Marriage is a Covenant, Not a Contract
A Foundation Worth Building On

In a world where promises are broken as quickly as they are made, the idea of marriage as a *covenant* has become increasingly unfamiliar. Many today view marriage as a legal contract, a mutual agreement based on terms, convenience, and performance. But God's view is different. His Word declares that marriage is a *sacred covenant,* not a civil contract. Understanding the difference between these two is essential if we desire a marriage that reflects heaven on earth.

The moment a man and a woman stand before God and declare their vows, something profound happens: *Heaven records a covenant.* This is not just a celebration or a ceremony; it is a divine joining. It is a holy transaction that binds two lives together in a spiritual, emotional, and physical union with God Himself as the eternal witness.

1. Covenant vs. Contract: What's the Difference?

A *contract* is built on mutual benefit and the protection of individual rights. If one party fails to meet the terms, the contract can be nullified. Contracts say, "I'll do my part if you do yours."

In contrast, a *covenant* is rooted in trust, unconditional love, and enduring faithfulness. A covenant says, "I will stay true to my vow regardless of your actions." In a covenant, the relationship itself is prioritized above personal satisfaction.

Think of this: A contract is written in ink. A covenant is written in blood. A contract is enforced by law. A covenant is upheld by love. A contract has loopholes. A covenant has no escape clause. A contract seeks fairness. A covenant seeks faithfulness.

Marriage is not a business arrangement. It is a spiritual bond that mirrors **Christ's relationship with the Church**, a bond built on sacrificial love and divine purpose.

2. God is the Witness and the Sustainer

Malachi 2:13–14 paints a sobering picture. God rebuked the men of Israel for dealing treacherously with their wives. He said:

"Because the Lord has been witness between you and the wife of your youth…"

This shows us that God is not a silent observer; He is actively involved in every marriage covenant. When a husband and wife exchange vows, *God is present, sealing and witnessing the agreement.*

Furthermore, the covenant is not sustained by human strength alone. God empowers the husband and wife with *grace, wisdom,* and *strength* to live out the vows made. Without Him, the covenant feels heavy. But with Him, it becomes a source of joy and purpose.

A threefold cord is not quickly broken (Ecclesiastes 4:12). When the husband and wife invite God into their union, they form a *triangular bond* that resists the attacks of the enemy. The marriage becomes more than emotional; it becomes spiritual, supernatural, and unshakeable.

3. A Covenant Reflects Christ and the Church

Paul gives one of the most powerful teachings on marriage in Ephesians 5:25-32. He compares the union of a husband and wife to *Christ's relationship with the Church:*

"Husbands, love your wives, just as Christ also loved the church and gave Himself for her..." (Ephesians 5:25)

This kind of love is not based on feelings or moods. It is based on sacrifice, patience, and grace. Christ gave Himself for the Church when she was still weak, immature, and even rebellious. This is the nature of covenantal love: it endures, it forgives, and it never gives up.

When a husband chooses to love his wife like Christ, and when a wife responds with reverence and support, they are living out the divine picture of redemption and restoration. The home becomes a small version of heaven. Children grow up witnessing Godliness in action. Friends and family are drawn to the peace that flows from that marriage.

4. Covenant Demands Lifelong Commitment

In today's culture, we see a growing pattern of temporary commitment. Many say, "If it doesn't work, just walk away." But that's not covenant thinking, that's contract thinking.

A covenant is a lifelong vow. It says, "For better or worse, for richer or poorer, in sickness and in health, I will remain by your side."

This kind of thinking produces stability, trust, and confidence. When both partners know they are *not* keeping one eye on the exit door, they feel safe to be vulnerable. Mistakes can be admitted. Flaws can be addressed. Growth can happen.

Remember this: *Covenant is not about perfection; it's about persistence.* You don't need to be perfect to have a heavenly marriage. You just need to keep showing up with humility, forgiveness, and love.

5. Covenant Love is Rooted in Forgiveness

One of the greatest strengths of a covenantal marriage is the ability to forgive deeply and consistently.

Forgiveness is the oxygen of covenant love. Without it, the relationship suffocates. But with it, the marriage breathes, heals, and thrives.

Jesus forgives us repeatedly, and we are called to do the same (Colossians 3:13): *"bearing with one another, and forgiving one another, if anyone has a complaint against another; even as Christ forgave you, so you also must do."*

In covenant marriage, spouses learn to say:

"I was wrong." "I'm sorry."
"Please forgive me." "Let's try again."

These words are not signs of weakness. They are signs of maturity and covenant understanding.

6. The Enemy Hates Covenant, but God Defends It

Marriage is a threat to the enemy's kingdom. When two people stand united in covenant, they can raise Godly children, support each other's purpose, serve in Ministry, and shine as lights in a dark world.

That's why the enemy works hard to distort the meaning of marriage, divide spouses, and destroy families. He wants people to think marriage is just a piece of paper. Yet, a covenant teaches us that challenges are opportunities for growth.

When couples turn to prayer, humility, and God's Word during crisis, the covenant is strengthened, not weakened. Storms don't break the marriage; they deepen the roots.

7. Walking in Covenant Daily

Living out the covenant is not a one-time vow; it's a daily decision. Each day, couples must:

Choose love over pride. Choose forgiveness over offense. Choose unity over ego. Choose prayer over silence. Choose faith over fear. It's about making *small daily choices* that reflect the larger vow. It's about living your "yes" every single day, even when it's hard. Let your marriage be a testimony that says, "So then, they are no longer two but one flesh. Therefore what God has joined together, let not man separate." (Matthew 19:6)

Renewing Your Covenant Today

No matter where your marriage stands today, whether it's flourishing or struggling, it's not too late to return to the heart of covenant. Take time to pray together. Read your vows aloud again. Invite the Holy Spirit to breathe fresh life into your union. Remember: a covenant marriage is not just about staying together; it's about growing together into the image of Christ.

As you embrace the power of covenant, you'll discover that marriage truly can be a heaven on earth, not because it's easy, but because it's holy.

CHAPTER 3

Building on the Rock: Christ as the Center of Your Marriage

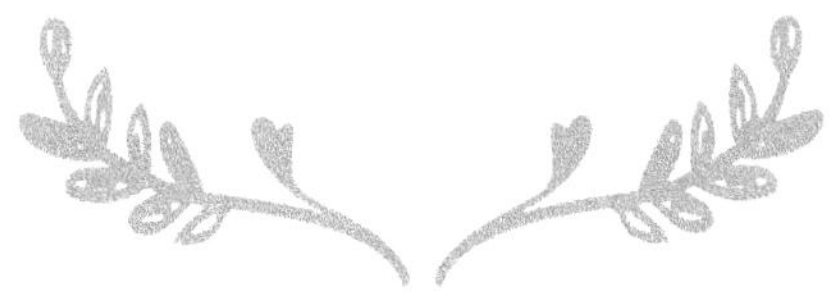

"For no other foundation can anyone lay than that which is laid, which is Jesus Christ." 1 Corinthians 3:11

The Strength of a Strong Foundation

Every building, whether a house, a marriage, or a life, needs a strong foundation. Jesus made this clear when He said that the wise man builds his house on the rock. When storms come, the house stands firm because its foundation is sure (Matthew 7:24–25). In the same way, a marriage that is not built on Jesus Christ will not survive the tests of life.

Many couples build their marriages on romance, beauty, money, or compatibility, but these things fade. The only lasting foundation for a strong, joyful, and enduring marriage is **Jesus Christ**.

1. Why Christ Must Be the Center

Jesus Christ is not just an addition to a Christian marriage; He is the cornerstone. Without Him, marriage becomes a struggle of human will. With Him, it becomes an alliance of divine purpose.

Christ gives love that never fails (1 Corinthians 13:8), He teaches forgiveness that restores, He models humility and service, He fills your home with peace. When both husband and wife place Christ at the center, their love becomes stronger, their purpose becomes clearer, and their union becomes unstoppable.

2. Marriage Is a Spiritual Institution

Marriage is not man-made; it is God-designed. Genesis 2:18–25 shows us that it was **God** who saw that Adam needed a helper. It was **God** who made Eve. It was **God** who brought her to Adam.

Therefore, it is only logical and spiritual wisdom that the One who created marriage must be the One who sustains it. Leaving God out of your marriage is like trying to operate a car without oil. It may look good on the outside, but friction will soon destroy the engine.

A Christ-centered marriage is not about attending Church on Sundays together. It's about: Praying together, studying God's Word together, serving each other as unto the Lord, submitting your plans and conflicts to God

3. Christ Teaches Servant Leadership and Mutual Honor

Ephesians 5:21 says, *"Submitting to one another in the fear of God."* This means both husband and wife are called to serve each other, not dominate or manipulate each other. Jesus Christ taught that true leadership is service (Mark 10:44–45). In a Christ-centered marriage:

The husband leads by loving, protecting, and providing; the wife supports by nurturing, encouraging, and honoring; Both prioritize the well-being of the other. There's no room for selfish ambition when Jesus is the center. He teaches us to wash each other's feet, to carry each other's burdens, and to speak truth in love.

4. Christ Gives Grace to Overcome Marital Challenges

Every marriage faces challenges. Even Godly couples go through storms sometimes. But Christ gives us grace and wisdom to overcome them.

2 Corinthians 12:9 says: *"My grace is sufficient for you, for My strength is made perfect in weakness."* When you hit a rough patch in your marriage, pray instead of complaining; wait on the Lord before reacting, and ask for God's wisdom instead of trusting your emotions. Couples who face trials with Christ grow stronger, more united, and more mature in love.

5. Christ Protects Your Marriage from Spiritual Attack

Marriage is more than a legal contract or emotional bond; it is a spiritual covenant instituted by God. Because of this, every Godly marriage becomes a target for the enemy; the devil despises anything that reflects the unity, love, and purpose of God. Marriage is one of the clearest pictures of Christ's love for His Church. Therefore, the attacks on Christian marriages are not just emotional or circumstantial; they are spiritual.

But praise be to God, Jesus Christ, the Head of every believing household, is also the divine protector of your marriage. His presence in your union is not passive. He actively watches over you and your spouse, shielding you from forces that seek to divide, discourage, or destroy.

Christ Is the Spiritual Covering Over Your Home

Just as the blood of the lamb protected the Israelites during the Passover, so too does the presence of Christ act as a covering over your home. When you invite Jesus Christ to be the center of your marriage, He surrounds you with His peace and charges His angels concerning you. His name becomes a shield that deflects the fiery darts of the enemy: miscommunication, resentment, infidelity, unforgiveness, fear, and more. *"The name of the Lord is a strong tower; the righteous run to it and are safe."* Proverbs 18:10.

Your marriage is safest when it is hidden in Christ.

Prayer and Spiritual Discernment as Weapons

Spiritual attacks often begin subtly, through irritation, offense, or emotional disconnection. But when Christ is Lord in your marriage, He alerts your spirit. He gives you discernment to identify what is natural and what is spiritual. You begin to see beyond the surface and realize that "we do not wrestle against flesh and blood" (Ephesians 6:12). You are not each other's enemies; there is a real enemy who wants to divide what God has joined.

As you pray together, Christ reinforces your unity. Prayer becomes the fortress where your love is protected, and your covenant is sealed afresh. Couples that pray together not only stay together, they also overcome together.

Christ Guards the Covenant

Marriage is not merely a promise between two people; it is a sacred covenant made before God. And because Jesus Christ is the mediator of a better covenant (Hebrews 8:6), He also defends it. He honors the vows you made before Him and empowers you by His Spirit to keep them. Even when one of you feels weak, He strengthens you. When temptation comes, He provides a way of escape (1 Corinthians 10:13). When disagreements arise, He sends His peace to calm the storm.

Christ Restores What the Enemy Tries to Steal

Even if your marriage has already faced attacks, like betrayal, pain, or broken trust, Christ is The Restorer. The enemy may come to steal, kill, and destroy, but Jesus comes that you may have life, and have it more abundantly (John 10:10). That includes abundant love, peace, and joy in your marriage. When you surrender the broken pieces of your relationship to Him, He can make all things new. He heals wounds, rebuilds trust, and revives the flame of love.

Submitting to Christ Closes the Door to the Enemy

A marriage that submits to Christ is a marriage that is sealed against demonic interference. As both husband and wife live under Christ's authority, they close the doors that sin, pride, or rebellion might open. Christ becomes the gatekeeper. No weapon formed against such a marriage can prosper (Isaiah 54:17), because Christ's Lordship is a wall of fire around it.

When Christ is at the center, your marriage is not just surviving; it is fortified. Instead of being torn apart by adversity, you will be drawn closer through every storm. Let Christ protect your marriage by keeping Him at the center, walking in prayer, and standing together in faith.

6. Practical Ways to Keep Christ at the Center

A Christ-centered marriage doesn't happen automatically; it must be cultivated with intentionality, prayer, and daily choices. When Christ is truly at the center, He becomes the Foundation upon which love, trust, and unity are built. Here are practical ways couples can actively keep Jesus at the center of their relationship:

Pray Together Regularly

Prayer is a lifeline for every Christian and a powerful unifier in marriage. Couples should make it a habit to pray together daily, whether in the morning, before meals, or at bedtime. Prayer invites God into your relationship, builds spiritual intimacy, and helps resolve issues in a Godly way. Praying together also teaches humility and mutual dependence on God.

"For where two or three are gathered together in My name, I am there in the midst of them." Matthew 18:20

Read the Word Together

The Bible is God's blueprint for life and relationships. Make it a point to read and discuss Scripture together. Choose a devotional plan or study a book of the Bible as a couple. Reflect on its meaning and ask how it applies to your relationship. The Word of God will shape your thinking, correct your attitudes, and align your marriage with God's will.

Worship as a Couple and Family

Attend church services together regularly. Worshipping as a family helps keep your focus on God and reinforces your shared faith. Join a local church where you can serve, grow spiritually, and be accountable. In addition, worshiping through songs, thanksgiving, and gratitude at home strengthens your spiritual atmosphere.

Serve God Together

Look for opportunities to serve God as a couple, whether in your local church, through missions, or by helping others in need. Serving together nurtures a heart of humility, compassion, and teamwork. It keeps your marriage from becoming self-focused and encourages you to reflect Christ's love.

Make Forgiveness a Lifestyle

Keeping Christ at the center requires a heart of forgiveness. Choosing to forgive as Christ forgives is the key. Remember, love keeps no record of wrongs. Forgiveness breaks the enemy's hold and restores unity. *"Be kind and compassionate to one another, forgiving each other, just as in Christ God forgave you."* Ephesians 4:32

Invite the Holy Spirit into Your Decisions

Before making decisions, big or small, pray and seek God's wisdom. Discuss your goals, plans, finances, and parenting through the lens of Scripture and with the guidance of the Holy Spirit. When Christ leads your decisions, peace and direction follow.

Guard Your Marriage Against Distractions

The world offers many distractions, busyness, careers, social media, and even well-meaning friendships that can pull you away from your spouse and from God. Protect your time together. Establish boundaries that safeguard your intimacy with each other and with Christ. Make room for meaningful conversations, shared devotion, and spiritual growth.

Encourage Each Other's Walk with Christ

A strong marriage is made of two strong individuals rooted in Christ. Encourage your spouse in their personal relationship with God. Support them in prayer, remind them of God's promises, and celebrate their spiritual victories. When both partners grow spiritually, the marriage naturally grows stronger.

Speak Life and God's Word over Each Other

Words are powerful. Speak blessings, encouragement, and Scripture over your spouse. Declare God's promises concerning your marriage. This not only builds your spouse's faith but also invites God's presence into your daily life together.

Keep Christ as the Ultimate Example of Love

Always look to Jesus as your model. His love is sacrificial, patient, kind, and enduring. Seek to love each other the way Christ loves the Church; with grace, mercy, and unconditional commitment.

Keeping Christ at the center of your marriage is not just about occasional acts of faith; it is about living every day with Jesus as your focus. When both partners are submitted to Christ, walking in love and truth, the marriage becomes a powerful testimony of God's design and beauty. A Christ-centered marriage is truly like heaven on earth.

7. Christ-centered Marriage Produces Godly Legacy

Your marriage is not just about the two of you; it's about generations. When you build your home on Christ, you're laying a foundation for your children and their children.

Psalm 127:1 says, *"Unless the Lord builds the house, they labor in vain who build it."*

Make your home a *training ground for righteousness*, a place where your children learn what it means to love, forgive, and live for Jesus. A home where Christ is exalted becomes a lighthouse in the neighborhood; a testimony to other couples, friends, and even unbelievers.

Build, Rebuild, or Reinforce Your Foundation

Whether you are newly married or have been together for decades, it's never too late to put Christ at the center. Even if cracks have formed in your marriage, Christ is the Master Builder. He can restore what is broken and strengthen what remains.

Remember, marriage is not just about surviving; it's about *thriving* in God's presence. Let your foundation be Jesus. Let your marriage reflect His love.

CHAPTER 4

Love Defined by God, Not the World

*"And now abide faith, hope, love, these three;
but the greatest of these is love." 1 Corinthians 13:13*

The Reality of Love

In today's culture, love is often confused with feelings, attraction, convenience, or even self-interest. Movies, social media, and even peer
advice define love as *what makes you happy* or *what you get out of a
relationship*. But this kind of love is fleeting. It changes with emotions,
circumstances, and appearances.

God's Word gives a different picture. True love is not based on feelings
or convenience; it is *rooted in God's character* and expressed through
faithful action, sacrifice, and commitment. Understanding God's defini-
tion of love is essential for a healthy, lasting marriage.

1. Love as a Choice, Not Just a Feeling

Emotions are unreliable. Feelings come and go; they fluctuate based on mood, stress, and circumstances. That's why a marriage built solely on feelings is fragile.

Godly love, however, is a decision. It is choosing to act in the best interest of your spouse; even when you don't feel like it. Ephesians 5:25 reminds husbands to *love their wives "just as Christ also loved the church and gave Himself for her."* Notice: Christ's love for the Church was *deliberate, sacrificial, and enduring*, not based on temporary feelings. Similarly, wives are called to love their husbands with respect, encouragement, and devotion (Ephesians 5:33). Love defined by God is active, not passive.

2. Love is Sacrificial

God's love is always sacrificial. It gives without expecting in return, forgives without limits, and prioritizes the well-being of others.

In marriage, this means: Putting your spouse's needs before your own, serving without complaints, forgiving quickly and genuinely, being patient and gentle, even in disagreement.

Sacrificial love creates trust and safety. When your spouse knows that your love is consistent and unwavering, it produces an environment where intimacy, honesty, and growth can flourish.

3. Love is Unconditional, Not Conditional

The world often teaches conditional love: *"I'll love you if you do this… or if you act that way…"* But God's love is unconditional (Romans 5:8). He loved us while we were still sinners, flawed, unfaithful, and broken.

In marriage, unconditional love means: Loving your spouse without condition, choosing forgiveness over resentment, staying committed through challenges, disappointments, and disagreements. This kind of love mirrors Christ's love for the Church. When both husband and wife embrace unconditional love, their marriage becomes a living testimony of God's faithfulness.

4. Love is Patient and Kind

1 Corinthians 13:4-7 defines love as this: *Love suffers long and is kind; love does not envy; love does not parade itself, is not puffed up; ⁵ does not behave rudely, does not seek its own, is not provoked, thinks no evil; ⁶ does not rejoice in iniquity, but rejoices in the truth; ⁷ bears all things, believes all things, hopes all things, endures all things."*

These qualities are not optional in marriage; they are *essential*. Patience allows couples to grow together. Kindness nurtures emotional safety. A love that imitates God's patience and kindness endures storms, misunderstandings, and external pressures.

5. Love is Committed Through Every Season

Worldly love often abandons relationships when they get hard. Godly love remains steadfast in seasons of financial difficulty, times of emotional struggle, moments of misunderstanding or conflict, and years when physical attraction changes. Commitment is a hallmark of God-defined love. It says, *"I am here for you always because God commands me to love you."*

6. Love is Expressed in Actions

Words alone are insufficient. Godly love requires tangible actions that communicate care, respect, and devotion. Examples include: Listening attentively, providing encouragement daily, praying together, supporting your spouse's dreams and goals, and acts of service without being asked. Marriage thrives when love is *visible, audible, and actionable*, not just professed verbally.

7. Love Overcomes the Lies of the World

The enemy constantly distorts the concept of love. He promotes self-ishness, comparison, instant gratification, and entitlement. But God's love challenges all of these: It chooses selflessness over self-interest; it rejoices in truth over deception; it endures challenges rather than fleeing from discomfort. A couple who embraces God-defined love can navigate challenges without losing sight of their eternal purpose.

8. Love Produces Unity and Intimacy

God's love binds hearts, aligns minds, and strengthens marriages. When love is centered on God, conflicts are resolved more easily, emotional connection deepens, spiritual intimacy grows, and Families experience peace and stability. Marriage becomes a partnership where each spouse is an encourager, supporter, and teammate in God's Kingdom.

9. Practical Steps to Grow Godly Love

Daily Devotion Together: Pray and read God's Word as a couple. *Regular Acts of Kindness:* Small, intentional gestures reinforce love. *Forgive Quickly:* Don't let bitterness accumulate. *Speak Life:* Encourage, bless, and affirm your spouse often. *Serve Each Other:* Look for ways to meet needs without being asked. *Reflect on God's Love:* Remind yourselves of His example in your marriage.

Love as God Intended

Worldly definitions of love are shallow, temporary, and conditional. But the love that God calls us to in marriage is deep, enduring, and transformative. It is love that gives, sacrifices, forgives, perseveres, and produces unity.

As you embrace God-defined love, your marriage can reflect heaven on earth. You won't just survive as a couple, you will thrive. Your home will be a sanctuary, your union a testimony, and your love a reflection of Christ Himself.

CHAPTER 5

The Role of Prayer in Marriage

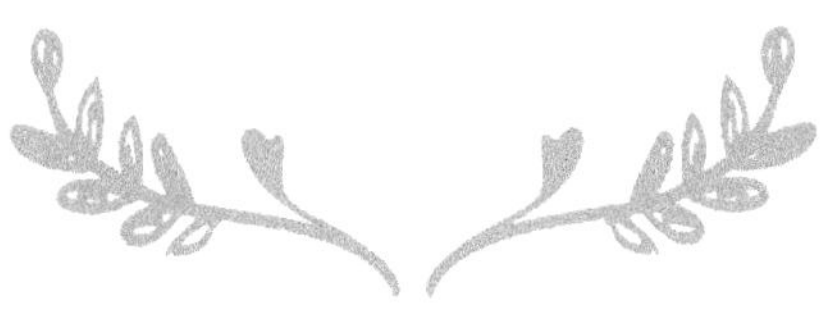

"Again I say to you, that if two of you agree on earth about anything that they ask, it will be done for them by My Father in heaven." Matthew 18:19

Why Prayer is the Heartbeat of Marriage

Prayer is more than a religious activity; it is the spiritual lifeline of a marriage. While love, communication, and commitment are vital, prayer is what connects a couple to the Ultimate source of wisdom, strength, and guidance: **God Himself**.

A marriage without prayer is like a lamp without oil: it may shine for a time, but eventually, darkness creeps in. Couples who pray together experience protection, unity, and spiritual intimacy that transcends human understanding.

Prayer in marriage is not only about asking God for blessings. It is about aligning your hearts, seeking His will, and allowing His power to work in and through your relationship.

1. Prayer Builds Spiritual Unity

Ecclesiastes 4:12 tells us that a "threefold cord is not quickly broken." In marriage, this threefold cord is God, husband, and wife. When a couple prays together:

Their hearts are aligned toward God's purposes. Conflicts are resolved with divine perspective. Decisions are made with wisdom and clarity. Prayer creates a shared spiritual vision, ensuring both spouses are moving forward together, not apart.

2. Prayer Protects Your Marriage

Marriage sometimes faces attacks from the enemy: misunderstandings, temptations, bitterness, and external pressures. Prayer acts as a *spiritual shield*, guarding your union from harm.

Pray for protection over your hearts, minds, and home. Pray against the schemes of the enemy that seek to sow division. Ask God to preserve your love, trust, and commitment.

James 5:16 *"Confess your trespasses to one another, and pray for one another, that you may be healed. The effective, fervent prayer of a righteous man avails much."* This verse encourages believers to *"pray for one another,"* emphasizing that consistent prayer strengthens relationships and spiritual resilience.

3. Prayer Deepens Love and Intimacy

When couples pray together, they share their hearts openly with God and with each other. This builds: Emotional intimacy, mutual understanding, compassion, and patience. Sharing prayer requests allows couples to see each other's vulnerabilities and joys. It creates a safe environment for love to grow and for wounds to heal.

4. Prayer Invites God's Guidance

God wants to be involved in every aspect of your marriage, big and small. Prayer invites His wisdom into your financial decisions, parenting strategies, career choices, and conflict resolution. Proverbs 3:5–6 reminds us: *"Trust in the Lord with all your heart, and lean not on your own understanding; in all your ways acknowledge Him, and He shall direct your paths."* Couples who pray together rely on God's guidance rather than their limited perspective.

5. Prayer Strengthens Forgiveness and Patience

One of the greatest benefits of a praying marriage is the ability to forgive. When you pray together, bitterness is replaced with grace, anger is softened by the Holy Spirit, past hurts are healed. Philippians 4:6–7 promises that prayer brings peace that surpasses understanding. This peace strengthens couples to forgive quickly and love patiently, reflecting Christ's love in their home.

6. Practical Ways to Pray as a Couple

Daily Devotionals: Begin and end your day together in prayer. Share your hearts and lift each other's needs.

Prayer Walks: Take time to walk and pray together. It creates an environment for both spiritual and emotional connection.

Intercessory Prayer: Pray for each other's personal growth, career, health, and spiritual life.

Scriptural Prayer: Use the Word of God to pray promises over your marriage. Examples include Ephesians 5:25, Colossians 3:14, and 1 Corinthians 13:4–7.

Praying During Conflict: Instead of arguing, pause and pray. Ask God to give perspective, calm emotions, and guide resolution.

7. Prayer Produces Fruit in Marriage

Couples who pray together consistently experience greater unity and understanding, emotional and spiritual intimacy, stronger resilience against temptations, joy, peace, and contentment in daily life, and a testimony that inspires others. Their home becomes a place of blessing, not just for themselves, but for friends, family, and community.

8. Prayer as a Lifestyle

Prayer should not be occasional or ritualistic; it should be a lifestyle. Couples who integrate prayer into every aspect of life discover that decisions become easier, conflicts are minimized, joy and gratitude increase, and God's purpose is revealed in their union. The couple that prays together stays together and their love grows beyond natural limitations.

Make Prayer the Heartbeat of Your Marriage

Prayer is the invisible thread that strengthens the marriage bond. It transforms ordinary love into heavenly love, resolves conflict before it escalates, and invites God's power to work in your union.

Commit today to make prayer a daily priority in your marriage. Pray for each other, pray with each other, and pray together. Let your marriage be a reflection of heaven on earth, a covenant strengthened by God's love and sustained by consistent communion with Him.

PART II
Spiritual Unity and Emotional Connection

CHAPTER 6

Becoming One Flesh: What It Truly Means

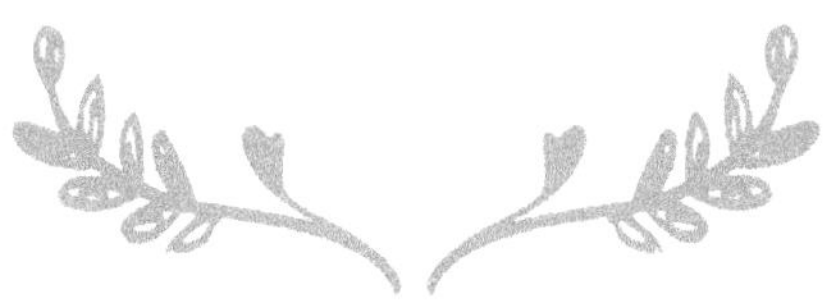

"Therefore a man shall leave his father and mother and be joined to his wife, and they shall become one flesh." Genesis 2:24

More Than Physical Union

When God declared in Genesis 2:24 that husband and wife *"shall become one flesh,"* He was revealing a mystery far deeper than physical intimacy. Many reduce this verse to the sexual aspect of marriage, but the concept of becoming one flesh is far richer. It speaks of unity in body, soul, and spirit.

To become one flesh means to move from two individuals living separately to one union living in covenant harmony, sharing life, dreams, burdens, and destiny. It is a merging of purpose under God's design.

1. The Spiritual Foundation of Oneness

Marriage was instituted by God, not by culture. The command to *"become one flesh"* is not optional; it is the divine blueprint for marital unity.

Jesus Christ reaffirms this in Matthew 19:6: *"So then, they are no longer two but one flesh. Therefore what God has joined together, let not man separate."* This unity is not something couples create by themselves; it is something *God joins together.* At the altar, He supernaturally fuses two lives into one covenant.

2. Leaving and Cleaving

Genesis 2:24 gives a clear order: *Leave:* A man shall leave his father and mother. *Cleave:* He shall be joined to his wife. *Become:* The two shall become one flesh.

The process of becoming one flesh starts *with leaving unhealthy dependence* on one's parents or past, then *cleaving* to one's spouse in loyalty, before *becoming* one in true unity. This doesn't mean abandoning family relationships but establishing *marriage as the new primary covenant.* Issues arise when spouses fail to "leave" emotionally, financially, or relationally, causing divided loyalties.

3. One Flesh in the Physical Sense

Sexual intimacy is God's sacred gift to marriage. It is both the celebration and the sealing of the covenant. Paul warns in 1 Corinthians 6:16: *"Do you not know that he who is joined to a harlot is one body with her? For 'the two,' He says, 'shall become one flesh.'"*

This shows that sexual union creates a bond that goes beyond the physical. That is why sex outside of marriage is destructive; it joins two people without a covenant. Within marriage, however, intimacy strengthens trust, affection, and unity.

God designed marital intimacy as a way *to deepen connection, heal divisions, and reflect love and vulnerability.* It is not just for procreation but for mutual joy, bonding, and unity.

4. One Flesh in the Emotional Sense

To be one flesh means sharing hearts openly. Couples are called to: communicate honestly, share dreams, fears, and joys, support each other emotionally, carry each other's burdens (Galatians 6:2)

Emotional intimacy requires vulnerability. Many marriages suffer because one or both partners build walls, hiding feelings, pain, or disappointments. But becoming one flesh means *tearing down those walls* and creating a safe space where both hearts are known and cherished.

5. One Flesh in the Spiritual Sense

True oneness cannot be achieved without God. Becoming one flesh means walking together spiritually, pursuing God's presence, praying as one, and living in obedience to His Word.

Amos 3:3 asks, *"Can two walk together, unless they are agreed?"* Spiritual unity ensures that the couple walks in the same direction toward Christ. When both spouses pursue God individually and together, their spirits align, producing deep unity.

6. The Process of Becoming One Flesh

Oneness is not achieved overnight; it is a *lifelong journey.* Couples may start marriage as two individuals with different backgrounds, habits, and perspectives. Over time, through love, communication, forgiveness, and prayer, they grow into deeper unity.

This process requires patience, growth takes time; forgiveness, mistakes can happen; grace, accepting each other's weaknesses; and intentionality, making choices that bring unity.

7. Barriers to Oneness

Several things hinder couples from becoming one flesh: Unforgiveness and bitterness, selfishness and pride, secrets and dishonesty, addiction or infidelity, excessive external influences (family, friends, career, etc.)

When these barriers are not addressed, unity is weakened. But through repentance, forgiveness, counseling, and prayer, couples can restore their covenant bond.

8. The Beauty of Oneness

When couples truly live as one flesh, their marriage radiates *Unity*: they stand together in decisions and direction. *Peace*: strife and division are minimized. *Strength*: together they resist trials and temptations. *Fruitfulness*: Their home becomes a fertile ground for raising Godly children. *Witness*: Their marriage reflects Christ and the Church to the world. This is the *heavenly picture* God intended: a union that reveals His glory and advances His Kingdom.

Practical Steps to Becoming One Flesh

Prioritize Time Together: Invest in shared moments daily. *Pray as One:* Invite God into your marriage constantly. *Resolve Conflicts Quickly:* Don't let anger linger overnight (Ephesians 4:26). *Protect Intimacy:* Guard your sexual and emotional bond from outside threats. *Be Transparent:* Share your heart, dreams, and struggles openly with each other. *Support Each Other's Purpose:* Celebrate and encourage each other's God-given calling.

One Flesh, One Destiny

Becoming one flesh is more than a biblical phrase; it is the very essence of marriage. It is God's design for unity, love, and togetherness. It is a journey of two becoming one in body, soul, and spirit. When you embrace oneness, you discover the joy of being truly united in purpose, passion, and faith. Your marriage becomes a testimony of Christ's love, a union that nothing can break, no enemy can divide, and no circumstance can shake.

Marriage is not about two people coexisting; it is about two people becoming one, for God's Glory in their shared destiny.

CHAPTER 7

The Power of Forgiveness and Grace

"Bearing with one another, and forgiving one another,
if anyone has a complaint against another; even as Christ
forgave you, so you also must do." Colossians 3:13

Why Forgiveness Is the Glue of Marriage

Two people living under one roof can clash sometimes. Words will be spoken in anger, expectations will be unmet, and mistakes can be made. But what separates strong marriages from broken ones is not the absence of conflict, but the *presence of forgiveness and grace.*

Forgiveness is the lifeline of every covenant relationship. Without it, resentment builds, hearts grow cold, and love is choked out by bitterness. Grace, on the other hand, is the atmosphere in which forgiveness thrives. It is the willingness to love and accept your spouse, not because they deserve it, but because God extended the same to you.

1. God's Example of Forgiveness

Marriage is meant to reflect Christ's relationship with His Church. In Ephesians 5, Paul compares the love of a husband for his wife to the sacrificial love of Christ. And what does Christ do? He forgives. He forgave Peter's denial. He forgave the woman caught in adultery. He forgave us while we were yet sinners (Romans 5:8). If Christ forgave us freely, can we withhold forgiveness from our spouse? Forgiveness in marriage is not optional; it is a command rooted in God's own character.

2. What Forgiveness Is (and Isn't)

To forgive does not mean to: *Excuse wrongdoing, deny the hurt, pretend it didn't happen, or allow repeated abuse without boundaries.* Rather, forgiveness means: Releasing your spouse from the debt they owe you and choosing not to hold their mistake against them. Refusing to allow bitterness to poison your heart and opening the door for healing and reconciliation.

Forgiveness does not mean erasing consequences, but it does mean refusing to let offense destroy covenant love.

3. The Poison of Unforgiveness

Unforgiveness in marriage breeds: *Bitterness*: Turning affection into coldness, *Distance*: Emotional walls that block intimacy, *Anger*: Explosions over small issues, *Resentment*: Keeping a record of wrongs (1 Corinthians 13:5). When unforgiveness lingers, small offenses turn into large mountains. A careless word becomes a source of years of bitterness. But forgiveness uproots these weeds before they destroy the marriage.

4. Grace: The Oil That Heals Relationships

Forgiveness is the act of letting go of offense; *grace is the lifestyle that makes forgiveness easier.* Grace means giving your spouse room to be human. It is loving them even when they are weak, flawed, or struggling. Romans 5:20 reminds us: *"But where sin abounded, grace abounded much more."* If God lavished grace on us, how much more should we extend it to the one we vowed to love "for better or worse"? Grace says, *"I will not expect perfection from you." "I will believe in your growth, even when you stumble." "I will choose love and mercy over judgment."*

5. Practical Steps to Forgiveness and Grace

Acknowledge the Hurt: Don't hide the pain. Be honest with yourself and your spouse. *Pray for Strength*: Forgiveness is not natural; it requires God's grace working in you. *Release the Offense:* Choose to let go, even if emotions linger. Forgiveness is an act of will, not a feeling. *Communicate Honestly:* Share what hurts you without blame or harshness. *Set Boundaries if Needed*: Grace does not mean tolerating abuse. Healthy love sets limits. *Rebuild Trust Gradually:* Forgiveness opens the door, but trust may take time to restore. *Keep Short Accounts:* Don't allow offenses to pile up. Resolve issues quickly (Ephesians 4:26).

6. Forgiveness Restores Intimacy

Couples often find that intimacy, emotional, spiritual, or physical, is restored after forgiveness. Resentment creates distance, but forgiveness closes the gap. A forgiven spouse feels safe, accepted, and loved, creating an atmosphere where closeness flourishes. Intimacy is hindered when hearts harbor bitterness. Many couples discover a breakthrough in this area only after releasing offenses and extending grace.

7. Forgiveness as a Daily Choice

Forgiveness is not a one-time act; it is a *daily decision.* Just as God's mercies are new every morning, couples must extend fresh grace every day. A strong marriage is built by two people who keep choosing forgiveness, not because the other is perfect, but because love is stronger than offense.

8. The Testimony of Forgiving Love

One of the most powerful witnesses of a Godly marriage is the ability to forgive and show grace. In a world that encourages divorce at the first sign of difficulty, couples who persevere through mistakes demonstrate the supernatural love of Christ. Forgiveness is not weakness; it is *strength clothed in humility*. It says, *"I choose covenant over conflict. I choose love over offense. I choose us over me."*

Forgiveness as the Language of Love

Marriage without forgiveness is impossible. Grace and forgiveness are the very language of love. They keep the covenant alive when storms come. When you forgive your spouse, you free both of you. You invite healing, restore intimacy, and reflect God's own heart. When you walk in grace, you create a marriage that breathes peace, joy, and hope. Remember: A strong marriage is not one without challenges; it is one where forgiveness and grace outshine every challenge.

A Modern Testimony of Forgiveness

I once counseled a couple, *John and Mary* (names changed), who came to me on the brink of divorce. John had made serious mistakes, broken trust, and financial irresponsibility. Mary carried deep wounds from years of disappointment. At first, she refused to forgive. "Pastor," she said with tears, "he doesn't deserve another chance." And she was right, he didn't. But neither do we deserve God's forgiveness, yet He lavishes it freely on us.

As Mary prayed and allowed the Holy Spirit to soften her heart, she made the choice to forgive, not because John earned it, but because Christ forgave her. Slowly, healing came. John repented and began rebuilding trust, while Mary walked in the freedom of releasing bitterness. Today, their marriage is not only restored but stronger. They often testify to other couples: *"Forgiveness saved our marriage. Without grace, we would not be together."*

9. Jesus Christ's Radical Teaching: Forgive Seventy Times Seven

Peter once asked Jesus, *"Lord, how many times shall I forgive my brother or sister who sins against me? Up to seven times?"* (Matthew 18:21). Peter thought he was being generous, but Jesus replied, *"I tell you, not seven times, but seventy-seven times."* In other words, forgiveness is not about keeping count. It is a lifestyle. In marriage, this means we do not forgive only once but continually. Forgiveness must flow as often as offenses arise, because love keeps no record of wrongs 1 Corinthians 13:5.

Grace in Action: A Story of Small Things

Not every act of forgiveness is about great betrayals. Often, it's the small, daily irritations that require grace. I recall a wife who was frustrated by her husband's forgetfulness. "He never remembers to put his socks in the laundry basket!" she said in exasperation. Though it seemed minor, resentment began to build.

Through prayer, she realized she needed to extend grace in even these small matters. Instead of nagging, she chose to laugh, forgive, and gently remind him. Over time, her lightheartedness softened their home, and what could have been a source of division became a reminder of grace. This illustrates a key truth: *forgiveness is not just for the big betrayals; it's for everyday life together.*

Living in Daily Forgiveness and Grace

A strong marriage is built when couples: Pray together, asking God for strength to forgive; speak words of grace instead of blame; keep short accounts by resolving conflict quickly (Ephesians 4:26); extend mercy for small irritations and big mistakes alike. Trust the Holy Spirit to heal wounds that seem impossible to overcome. Grace and forgiveness do not minimize sin, but they maximize love. As Paul wrote in Colossians 3:14, *"And over all these virtues put on love, which binds them all together in perfect unity."* Forgiveness and grace are not optional; they are the very heartbeat of a Godly marriage.

CHAPTER 8

Respect, Honor, and Submission

"Submitting to one another in the fear of God." Ephesians 5:21

The Missing Pillar in Many Marriages

Many marriages struggle not because love is absent, but because respect and honor are neglected. Love may be the foundation, but without respect, it quickly crumbles. God's design for marriage includes a balance of love, respect, and mutual submission.

In Ephesians 5, Paul gives a divine order: husbands are called to love their wives as Christ loves the Church, and wives are called to respect their husbands. But before he gives these distinct instructions, he begins with a powerful statement in verse 21: *"Submit to one another in the fear of God."* This shows us that mutual submission is the heartbeat of a Godly marriage. It is not about competition or domination, but about serving each other in humility and reverence for God.

1. Understanding Respect in Marriage

Respect is more than politeness; it is a *deep regard for the worth and dignity of your spouse*. For a wife, respect means: Honoring her husband's leadership; valuing his efforts and provision; speaking to him with gentleness, not contempt; trusting his decisions when aligned with God's Word

For a husband, respect means: Valuing his wife's voice and opinions; Affirming her worth, not belittling her; Protecting her from harm; Recognizing her as a co-heir of God's grace, 1 Peter 3:7. Respect must be mutual, not one-sided. When one spouse consistently feels dishonored, the marriage loses its harmony.

2. The Role of Honor in Marriage

To honor means to *esteem, elevate, and treat as precious*. In 1 Peter 3:7, husbands are commanded to "honor" their wives as the weaker vessel, meaning not lesser in value, but delicate and deserving of care.

Honor in marriage looks like: Publicly speaking well of your spouse; Avoiding comparison with others; Celebrating their strengths instead of magnifying weaknesses; Defending their dignity even in their absence.

A marriage without honor becomes toxic. But when spouses honor each other, they create an atmosphere of security and joy.

3. What Is Mutual Submission?

Submission in the Bible often stirs debate, but when understood correctly, it is liberating. Submission does not mean inferiority; it means *order and humility under God's design*. Mutual submission means both husband and wife put each other's needs above their own. It is serving one another with Christlike humility. It is laying down pride, selfishness, and ego for the sake of unity.

Jesus Christ modeled submission by saying in John 6:38: *"For I have come down from heaven, not to do My own will, but the will of Him who sent Me."* If Christ could submit in love, then in marriage, submission should be seen as a strength, not a weakness.

4. Husbands: Leading Through Love

God calls husbands to lead as *servant leaders*. Leadership in marriage is not about control but responsibility. A husband leads by sacrificial love Ephesians 5:25. He leads by example, not by force. He creates an environment where his wife feels safe, valued, and cherished. True leadership inspires submission naturally. A wife finds it easier to respect and follow a husband who loves like Christ: selflessly, consistently, and sacrificially.

5. Wives: Empowering Through Respect

The greatest need of a man is not always love, but *respect*. When a wife respects her husband, she fuels his confidence and leadership. Conversely, constant disrespect can crush a man's spirit and lead him away from his calling.

Respect does not mean silence or passivity. It means: Using words that build up, not tear down. Trusting him enough to allow him to lead. Offering wise counsel without nagging. Showing appreciation for his efforts, even small ones. A respectful wife does not lose her voice, she uses it with wisdom.

6. The Balance of Love and Respect

Ephesians 5:33 beautifully summarizes the balance:

"Nevertheless let each one of you in particular so love his own wife as himself, and let the wife see that she respects her husband." Marriage thrives when husbands lead with *love* and wives respond with *respect*.

But when love is absent, respect fades. And when respect is absent, love grows cold. Both are needed, and both should flow from mutual submission to Christ.

7. Barriers to Respect, Honor, and Submission

Pride and selfishness: Insisting on one's own way. *Unforgiveness:* Holding past mistakes against your spouse. *Cultural misconceptions:* Twisting submission into oppression. *Comparison:* Measuring your spouse against others. *Neglect:* Refusing to show appreciation daily. These barriers must be torn down to allow biblical respect and honor to flourish.

8. Practical Ways to Show Respect, Honor, and Submission

Pray Together; Start each day submitting to God as a couple. *Speak Life;* Make it a habit to encourage, not criticize. *Serve Each Other;* Look for daily opportunities to meet each other's needs. *Decide Together;* Practice joint decision-making in major areas. *Guard Against Pride.* Remember, marriage is not "me first," but "we together." *Celebrate Each Other Publicly;* Never despise your spouse in front of others. *Practice Active Listening;* Respect your spouse by hearing their heart fully.

A Marriage of Mutual Honor

Respect, honor, and submission are not outdated concepts; they are the very keys to a thriving, Christ-centered marriage. A couple that lives by these principles reflects the relationship between Christ and the Church: love that sacrifices, respect that uplifts, and submission that glorifies God. When both husband and wife choose humility over pride, service over selfishness, and honor over dishonor, their marriage becomes unshakable.

A Godly marriage is not a battlefield of who is greater; it is a union of mutual love, respect, and submission in reverence to God.

CHAPTER 9

Healing Past Wounds Together

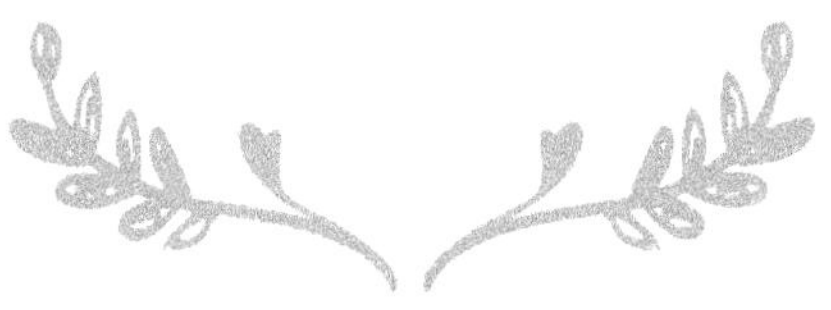

"He heals the brokenhearted and binds up their wounds." Psalm 147:3

The Baggage We Bring into Marriage

Every marriage begins with two people who bring not only their hopes and dreams but also their past experiences and hurts. Some wounds are small; others run deep: rejection from childhood, betrayal from past relationships, family dysfunction, trauma, or mistakes we made ourselves.

If these wounds are not addressed, they can silently shape how we communicate, trust, and love. Many conflicts in marriage are not really about the present moment but about *unhealed pain from the past*. The good news is that God has provided healing through Christ, and marriage can become a safe place where both husband and wife experience restoration *together*.

1. Recognizing the Reality of Wounds

The first step in healing is acknowledging that wounds exist. Some couples pretend nothing is wrong, hiding pain under silence, busyness, or superficial peace. But what is hidden will eventually surface.

Signs of unresolved wounds include: Overreacting to small issues. Difficulty trusting your spouse fully. Withdrawing emotionally during conflict. Comparing your spouse to someone from the past. Carrying anger and bitterness. Ignoring these wounds does not make them disappear; it only delays healing. A Christ-centered marriage provides a safe space to bring these wounds into the light.

2. Christ, the True Healer

While spouses can support one another, true healing comes from God. Psalm 147:3 promises that the Lord heals the brokenhearted and binds up their wounds. Jesus is not only the Savior of our souls but also the Restorer of our hearts. Isaiah 53:5 says: *"By His Stripes we are healed."* In marriage, both husband and wife must continually look to Christ for healing. Prayer, worship, and Scripture invite His healing power into the marriage, transforming wounds into testimonies.

3. Choosing Vulnerability Over Silence

Healing requires vulnerability. James 5:16 instructs: *"Confess your trespasses to one another, and pray for one another, that you may be healed."* This does not mean exposing every painful memory at once, but it does mean creating a safe environment where honesty is welcomed, not judged. Vulnerability allows spouses to share their struggles openly, admit their fears and insecurities, and express past hurts that still influence the present. When vulnerability is met with *love, patience, and prayer*, healing begins to flow.

4. Practicing Forgiveness Together

Unforgiveness is one of the greatest barriers to healing. Whether the wound comes from your spouse or from your past, holding on to bitterness poisons intimacy. Forgiveness does not mean ignoring pain or pretending it never happened. It means: Releasing the offender to God's judgment, refusing to let bitterness control your heart, choosing peace over resentment. Colossians 3:13 says: *"Bear with each other and forgive one another if any of you has a grievance against someone. Forgive as the Lord forgave you."* Forgiving together as a couple creates freedom, not only for the wounded partner but also for the marriage.

5. Praying Over Each Other's Wounds

Prayer is a powerful tool for healing in marriage. When a spouse prays over the other's pain, it communicates: *"You are not alone. I stand with you, and I will carry this with you before God."* Pray specifically: For emotional scars to be healed, for the Holy Spirit to replace fear with peace, for God's truth to replace lies from the past, and for strength to forgive and move forward. This act of intercession brings spiritual intimacy and invites God's presence into areas of pain.

6. Replacing Lies with God's Truth

Past wounds often leave people believing lies. But God's Word declares the opposite: *"You are fearfully and wonderfully made."* Psalm 139:14; *"I will never leave you nor forsake you."* Hebrews 13:5; *"Love never fails."* 1 Corinthians 13:8; *"If anyone is in Christ, he is a new creation."* 2 Corinthians 5:17. As a couple, replace lies with truth. Speak God's promises over each other. Let the Word of God reshape your identity and your view of love.

7. Creating a Healthy Environment at Home

Healing is not only about moments of prayer, but also about cultivating a daily environment where healing can thrive. A healthy home is one where: Words of affirmation replace criticism, laughter replaces heaviness, patience replaces harshness, and encouragement replaces comparison. Small daily actions, kind words, thoughtful gestures, and listening without judgment are like medicine for the heart.

8. When Professional Help Is Needed

Sometimes wounds are too deep to process alone. In such cases, seeking Godly counseling is not a sign of weakness but of wisdom. Christian counselors, pastors, or mentors can provide tools and biblical insight to help couples navigate complex pain. Remember: healing is a process. It may take time, but with patience and support, even the deepest wounds can become places of strength.

From Wounds to Testimonies

No marriage is free from the impact of past wounds. But God has not called us to remain broken; He has called us to be healed and to walk in freedom. As husband and wife face wounds *together*, relying on Christ, practicing forgiveness, and speaking truth, their pain can become a testimony of God's grace. What the enemy intended for destruction becomes a platform for victory. A healthy marriage is a strong one. It is a marriage where two hearts, once scarred, now beat as one, strengthened by love and sustained by God.

CHAPTER 10

The Marriage Altar
Praying as a Couple

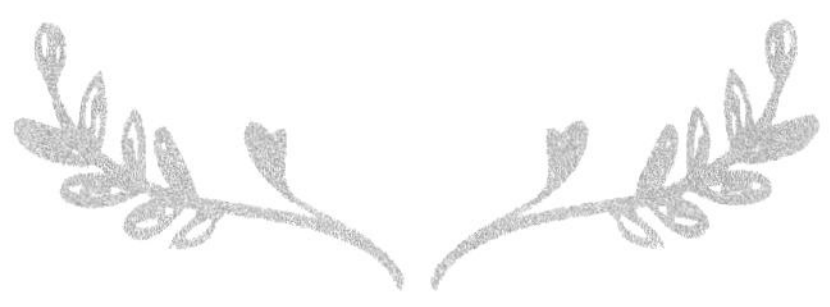

"Then the Lord God took the man and put him in the garden of Eden to tend and keep it." Genesis 2:15

"If two of you agree on earth concerning anything that they ask, it will be done for them by My Father in heaven." Matthew 18:19

The Altar at Home

Every marriage needs an *altar;* a place and practice of prayer where husband and wife meet God together. In the Old Testament, altars were built as places of worship, sacrifice, and communion with God. They were places of covenant, remembrance, and power.

In the same way, the "marriage altar" is not just symbolic; it is a spiritual discipline where couples come together before God, invite His presence, and dedicate their relationship to His purposes.

Too many marriages today are weak because the altar at home is broken or missing. Couples eat together, sleep together, and work together, but they do not pray together. Yet, praying as a couple is one of the most powerful spiritual tools for strengthening love, unity, and protection in marriage.

1. Why a Marriage Altar is Necessary

It invites God into the marriage daily. Prayer ensures God is not a distant guest but the permanent resident in your home. *It aligns hearts and minds.*

When you pray together, misunderstandings fade, and unity increases. *It builds intimacy.*

Sharing spiritual burdens and joys deepens emotional and spiritual connection. *It brings divine protection.*

A praying couple is harder for the enemy to divide or defeat. Without a prayer altar, couples may drift apart spiritually even while living under the same roof.

2. Biblical Power of Agreement in Prayer

Jesus Christ declared in Matthew 18:19, *"If two of you agree on earth concerning anything that they ask, it will be done for them by My Father in heaven."*

Marriage gives you a built-in prayer partner. Agreement in prayer releases supernatural results. When husband and wife come into unity, their prayers carry multiplied authority. This is why the devil works hard to create division; he knows that agreement in prayer makes couples unstoppable.

3. What Happens at the Marriage Altar

At the altar of prayer, couples experience *cleansing* as they confess and forgive one another. *Covering*: As they intercede for their home, children, work, and ministry. *Consecration*: As they dedicate their goals, finances, and future to God. *Closeness*: As they grow in intimacy with each other and with Christ. The altar is where love is rekindled, trust is restored, and divine wisdom is released.

4. Hindrances to the Marriage Altar

Many couples struggle to pray together because of: *Busyness*: Packed schedules leave no time. *Disunity*: Quarrels or unresolved conflicts block prayer. *Pride*: One or both spouses resist vulnerability. *Spiritual laziness*: Lack of discipline in prayer. 1 Peter 3:7 warns that when husbands fail to honor their wives, their prayers are hindered. Likewise, bitterness and pride can close the heavens over a marriage. Clearing these obstacles is vital for a strong marriage altar.

5. Building and Sustaining Your Marriage Altar

Set a Time: Choose a regular time to pray together, morning, evening, or both. *Keep it Simple*: Start small. Pray short prayers together, then grow into longer sessions. *Use the Word*: Pray Scriptures over your marriage, children, and circumstances. *Include Worship*: Sing, praise, or thank God together; it strengthens unity. *Be Honest*: Share real struggles, fears, and dreams with God and with each other. *Be Consistent*: Even five minutes daily is better than long but irregular prayers. Over time, your altar will grow into a sacred routine that anchors your marriage.

6. Topics to Pray About as a Couple

Love and unity in your marriage. *Protection* from temptation and the enemy. *Wisdom* for decisions in family, finances, and ministry. *Your children*, for salvation, protection, and purpose. *Your spiritual growth*, to walk in holiness and service. *Your calling as a couple* to be a light in your community.

7. Testimony of Couples Who Pray Together

Research, as well as countless testimonies, show that couples who pray together experience: Lower rates of divorce, greater emotional intimacy, better conflict resolution, and stronger family bonds. One couple once shared: *"Every time we were on the verge of a serious argument, we paused to pray. Sometimes we prayed with tears, other times in silence. But prayer always softened our hearts, and the fight lost its power."* This is the beauty of the marriage altar; it breaks the enemy's weapons and restores peace.

8. The Marriage Altar as Ministry

Your marriage altar doesn't just bless you, it impacts others. A praying couple becomes: A covering for their children, a testimony to other families, an intercessory force for their church and community. When couples pray faithfully, God uses their unity to release blessings beyond their home. Your altar becomes a *spiritual lighthouse*.

Restore the Altar

Just as Elijah repaired the broken altar on Mount Carmel (1 Kings 18:30), many marriages today need to *rebuild the altar of prayer*. Without it, marriage becomes vulnerable to storms. With it, your love becomes unshakeable, your home becomes a sanctuary, and your marriage reflects heaven on earth.

Start where you are. Pray together today. Let your marriage altar burn with the fire of the Holy Spirit and watch how God transforms your home.

PART III

Communication and Conflict

CHAPTER 11

Learning to Truly Listen

"So then, my beloved brethren, let every man be swift to hear, slow to speak, slow to wrath." James 1:19

Listening: The Forgotten Skill in Marriage

Many couples think the biggest problem in communication is *not talking enough*. But in truth, the greater problem is *not listening enough*. Listening is not the same as hearing. Hearing is a biological process; your ears capture sound. Listening, however, is *intentional*; it requires attention, empathy, and humility. In marriage, *listening is love in action.*

When a spouse feels unheard, they also feel unloved. But when you truly listen, you are saying, *"You matter. Your words, your feelings, your heart are important to me."*

1. The Biblical Call to Listen

God is the greatest Listener. The Bible is filled with assurances like: *"Call to Me, and I will answer you..."* (Jeremiah 33:3). *"The Lord has heard the voice of my weeping.*" (Psalm 6:8). "*The righteous cry out, and the Lord hears…*" (Psalm 34:17)

If God, Who already knows everything, listens to His children, how much more should spouses listen to one another? James 1:19 sets the foundation: "*Be swift to hear, slow to speak, slow to wrath.*" Imagine how many marital conflicts would dissolve if this verse were applied daily.

2. Why Listening is Hard

Listening is not natural for most people. Instead of listening, we: *Prepare our reply* while the other is still talking. *Defend ourselves* instead of understanding. *Interrupt* because we think we already know. *Dismiss feelings* because they don't make sense to us. Pride, impatience, and distractions make it difficult to truly listen. But without listening, communication breaks down and conflict starts.

3. The Heart of Listening: Seeking to Understand

Most people do not listen with the intention of understanding; they listen with the intent to reply. True listening in marriage means: *Pausing judgment* until your spouse has finished. *Hearing both words and emotions.* Sometimes what your spouse is saying is less important than how they are feeling. *Entering their perspective.* You don't have to agree to understand. Proverbs 20:5 reminds us: "*Counsel in the heart of man is like deep water, but a man of understanding will draw it out.*" Listening is how you draw out the heart of your spouse.

4. How to Practice Active Listening in Marriage

Here are biblical and practical steps to become a better listener: *Give full attention.* Put away the phone, TV remote, or laptop. Make eye contact. *Use affirming body language.* Nod, smile, or respond with small words like "I see" or "Go on." *Do not interrupt.* Proverbs 18:13 warns against answering before hearing the whole matter. *Reflect.*

Repeat in your own words: *"So what I hear you saying is…"* This shows you understood. *Validate feelings.* Even if you disagree, acknowledge emotions: *"I understand you feel hurt about this."* *Ask clarifying questions.* Instead of assuming, say: *"Can you explain more about what you meant?"* *Respond with grace.* Once they finish, reply calmly and respectfully. Listening is an *art of humility*; it says, *"Your heart is more important than my opinion."*

5. Barriers to Listening in Marriage

Some of the greatest obstacles are: *Pride:* Believing your perspective is the only one that matters. *Anger:* When tempers flare, ears close. *Busyness:* Rushing through conversations instead of giving time. *Assumptions:* Thinking you already know what your spouse will say.

To overcome these, couples must intentionally slow down and choose patience over pride.

6. The Fruit of Truly Listening

When couples develop the discipline of listening, they experience: *Deeper intimacy:* Listening makes your spouse feel safe and valued. *Reduced conflict:* Many arguments end quickly when one spouse simply listens. *Better problem-solving:* Solutions arise when both voices are heard. *Spiritual growth:* Listening breeds humility, patience, and self-control.

Proverbs 15:1 says: *"A soft answer turns away wrath."* Often, the softest answer is *listening quietly* before speaking.

7. Practical Exercises for Couples

Daily Check-In: Spend 10–15 minutes daily just sharing about your day, without distractions. One talks, the other only listens. *Listening Challenge:* For one week, agree that whenever conflict arises, one person speaks while the other repeats back what they heard before responding. *Prayer:* After praying together, spend a few minutes silently asking God to help you listen better to your spouse.

8. Listening as Ministry

Your listening ear can become healing for your spouse's heart. Sometimes what they need is not advice, but a safe place to unload. By listening, you minister comfort, encouragement, and love. This mirrors Christ, who calls Himself the *"Wonderful Counselor"* (Isaiah 9:6). Counselors heal not by talking more but by listening deeply.

Ears That Love

A strong marriage is built not only on spoken words but on *listening hearts.* True listening is not weakness; it is love in its most humble form. James 1:19 is the golden rule for couples: *"Be swift to hear, slow to speak, slow to wrath."* If both husband and wife embrace this, their communication will flourish, conflict will lessen, and their love will deepen. So, choose today to give your spouse the gift of your ears. In marriage, *listening is one of the loudest ways to say "I love you."*

CHAPTER 12

Forgiveness, The Oil of Marriage

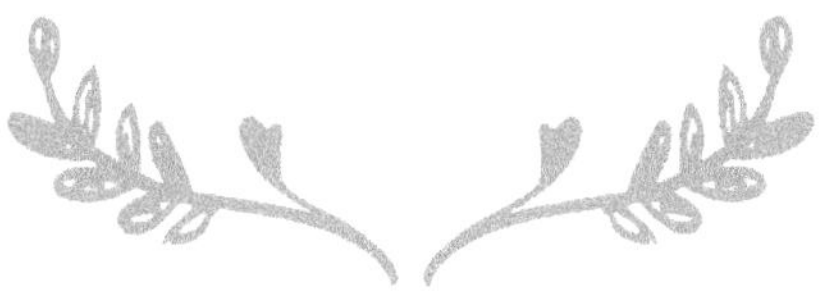

"And be kind to one another, tenderhearted, forgiving one another, even as God in Christ forgave you." Ephesians 4:32

Why Forgiveness is Essential

Marriage is a Divine union, but it is also a human relationship. And because we are human, mistakes, offenses, and misunderstandings are inevitable. Even the most loving couples might hurt each other, sometimes unintentionally, sometimes through careless words or actions.

Without forgiveness, these wounds intensify, creating bitterness, resentment, and a distance between spouses. Forgiveness is the *oil that keeps the gears of marriage running smoothly.* It lubricates the friction that naturally arises when two people live closely together. Just as oil in a machine, forgiveness prevents marriage from breaking down under the strain of offenses.

1. Understanding Forgiveness in Marriage

Many people misunderstand forgiveness. They think forgiveness is forgetting the offense, pretending it didn't happen, or excusing wrong behavior. True forgiveness is *choosing to release the offender from the debt they owe you*, while acknowledging the hurt and choosing love over revenge.

Forgiveness is not optional in a covenant marriage; it is commanded by God. Jesus Christ said in Matthew 18:21-22: *"I tell you, not seven times, but seventy-seven times."* This teaches us that forgiveness is not a one-time act; it is a continual practice, a lifestyle, and a spiritual discipline.

2. Forgiveness Reflects God's Heart

God's forgiveness is the ultimate example. Colossians 3:13 reminds us: *"Bear with each other and forgive one another if any of you has a grievance against someone. Forgive as the Lord forgave you."* When a husband forgives his wife, or a wife forgives her husband, they are reflecting the *heart of Christ*. Forgiveness is a spiritual act, not just an emotional one. It releases the power of resentment and allows God's love to flow through the relationship.

Forgiveness doesn't just heal the one who is forgiven; it heals the one who forgives. Unforgiveness is like carrying a heavy backpack full of stones. Each unresolved offense is a stone, weighing down your heart, mind, and soul. Forgiveness sets you free.

3. The Consequences of Unforgiveness

When forgiveness is absent, marriage suffers in multiple ways: *Bitterness grows;* A small hurt left unresolved becomes a grudge in the home. *Communication breaks down:* Walls go up, leaving spouses isolated and misunderstood. *Intimacy fades:* Love cannot flourish where resentment dominates. *Spiritual vulnerability increases:* Unforgiveness opens the door for the enemy to plant division and strife. Ephesians 4:31 warns us: *"Get rid of all bitterness, rage and anger, brawling and slander, along with every form of malice."* Every bit of unforgiveness in a marriage gives the enemy a foothold. Forgiveness, however, restores peace, strengthens trust, and fortifies the covenant.

4. Forgiveness is a Choice, Not a Feeling

Many people wait until they feel like forgiving. But forgiveness is a *decision of the will,* not a fluctuating emotion. Feelings often lag behind faith. You may not feel like forgiving, but God calls you to choose forgiveness as an act of obedience.

Practical steps to choose forgiveness: *Acknowledge the hurt:* Don't minimize or deny your feelings. *Decide to forgive:* Declare in prayer that you release the debt the offender owes you. *Pray for your spouse:* Ask God to bless them, even as you release your hurt. *Move forward:* Let go of the incident, and don't bring it up repeatedly as ammunition in arguments.

Remember, forgiveness is not a weakness. It is spiritual strength and a weapon of love.

5. Forgiveness Restores Love and Intimacy

Forgiveness is closely tied to emotional and spiritual intimacy. When forgiveness flows, resentment disappears, and the couple is free to love fully again. It creates an environment where confessions can be made without fear, affection and romance are restored, partnership in life, ministry, and parenting thrives, and children witness the power of God's grace in action. Think of forgiveness as the oil in a lamp. Without it, the flame sputters. With it, the flame burns bright, providing warmth, light, and comfort to the entire household.

6. Forgiveness in Action: Real-Life Examples

Consider a husband who constantly criticizes his wife's efforts. She feels unappreciated and hurt. Instead of retaliating or storing resentment, she chooses forgiveness. She prays for him, speaks to him with love, and lets go of the offense. Over time, he notices her gentle spirit and begins to change, responding with kindness. Forgiveness not only heals the wound, it transforms hearts.

Similarly, a wife who hurts her husband through careless words can ask for forgiveness and make restitution. When both practice forgiveness consistently, small offenses don't escalate into bitterness.

7. Forgiveness as a Daily Discipline

Forgiveness is not just for major offenses; it is a daily discipline. Every day slight misunderstandings and irritations require constant forgiveness. A marriage that practices daily forgiveness will have fewer conflicts, deeper peace, and stronger unity. Try this practical habit: *Every night, review your day and release any minor grievances.* Pray together, even for small hurts, and keep the heart soft. This habit keeps the marriage lubricated and prevents small problems from becoming mountains.

8. Forgiveness Opens the Door to God's Blessing

Forgiveness is a key to unlocking God's blessings in marriage. Jesus said in Matthew 6:14: *"For if you forgive men their trespasses, your heavenly Father will also forgive you."* God blesses marriages where forgiveness flows freely. These homes are marked by peace that surpasses understanding, stability, growth in spiritual maturity, joy, laughter, and intimacy that reflect God's heart. Forgiveness transforms ordinary marriages into *heavenly homes*, where the Spirit of God resides and love grows exponentially.

Make Forgiveness Your Daily Oil

Forgiveness is the *oil of marriage.* It lubricates the friction, removes bitterness, restores intimacy, and strengthens the covenant bond. Without it, marriages grind to a halt under the weight of resentment. With it, couples experience joy, peace, and God's supernatural presence.

Make a commitment today: choose forgiveness every day. Release offenses, pray for your spouse, and trust God to heal hearts. A marriage filled with forgiveness is a marriage filled with *love*; a home where grace flows freely, hearts are united, and God is glorified.

CHAPTER 13

Resolving Conflicts with Godly Wisdom

"A soft answer turns away wrath, but a harsh word stirs up anger." Proverbs 15:1

Turning Conflict into Growth

Even the most loving, committed couples may experience disagreements. The question is not *if* conflict will arise, but *how* it is handled. Many marriages break down not because couples disagree, but because they *handled disagreement wrongly*, with anger, withdrawal, or manipulation.

Conflict, however, is not the enemy of marriage. When addressed with wisdom, it can become a tool for growth, understanding, and deeper intimacy. Resolving conflict with Godly wisdom transforms a fight into an opportunity for mutual respect, communication, and spiritual maturity.

1. Understanding the Root of Conflict

Before attempting to resolve a conflict, it is crucial to understand its root cause. Often, disagreements are not about the surface issue; they are about unmet needs, unhealed wounds, or differing expectations.

Example: John and Mary constantly argued about finances. On the surface, it seemed like a dispute over budgeting. But after prayer and reflection, they realized the root was fear. John feared scarcity, while Mary feared lack of freedom. Recognizing the underlying emotional triggers allowed them to resolve the conflict without resentment. James 4:1 asks, *"Where do wars and fights come from among you? Do they not come from your desires for pleasure that war in your members?"* Conflicts often reveal deeper desires, insecurities, or sins that need addressing with God's guidance.

2. Seek God First

Before speaking or reacting, take time to pray and seek God's wisdom. Proverbs 3:5-6 remind us: *"Trust in the Lord with all your heart, and lean not on your own understanding; in all your ways acknowledge Him, and He shall direct your paths."* Many couples make the mistake of reacting emotionally, which often escalates conflict. Instead, pause and ask: What is God trying to teach me in this situation? How can I respond in a way that honors Him and my spouse?

Example: Linda was angry with her husband for forgetting her birthday. Instead of yelling, she spent time in prayer, asking God to help her respond with grace. When she spoke, she calmly expressed her feelings, and her husband apologized sincerely. The conflict turned into a deeper conversation about love language and attentiveness.

3. Speak the Truth in Love

Ephesians 4:15 instructs, *"But speaking the truth in love, may grow up in all things into Him who is the head—Christ."* Resolving conflict requires honesty, not harshness. Harsh words wound; gentle, loving words heal.

Practical Steps: Use "I" statements instead of "You" statements. ("I feel hurt when…" instead of "You never…"). Avoid blaming. Focus on feelings and solutions. Maintain a soft tone, even when discussing hard truths.

4. Listen Actively

Listening is as important as speaking. Many conflicts escalate because *one or both partners stop listening.* Godly wisdom requires seeking to understand before being understood (Proverbs 18:13).

Tips for Active Listening: Make eye contact and avoid distractions. Repeat what your spouse said to ensure understanding. Ask clarifying questions without judgment. Avoid interrupting or planning your rebuttal while they speak.

Example: Sophie felt her husband didn't respect her opinions. During a disagreement, he practiced active listening by repeating her concerns and asking follow-up questions. Sophie felt heard and responded without anger. They discovered solutions that satisfied both their needs.

5. Agree to Pause if Needed

Sometimes, emotions run too high to resolve conflict immediately. Proverbs 14:29 teaches: *"He who is slow to wrath has great understanding, but he who is impulsive exalts folly."* Agreeing to pause does not mean avoiding the issue. It allows tempers to cool and hearts to align with God before discussing further.

Example: During a heated argument about parenting, Paul and Anna chose to pause, pray separately for a day, and then reconvene in the evening with calm hearts. This prevented hurtful words and allowed productive problem-solving.

6. Seek Forgiveness and Extend Grace

Conflicts often leave emotional scars. Resolving conflict requires mutual humility: asking for forgiveness and extending it freely. *Forgive quickly:* Don't let resentment fester. *Take responsibility:* Admit your mistakes even if partially responsible. *Show grace:* Understand that your spouse, like you, can make mistakes sometimes.

Example: Rachel and David argued over time management. David apologized for not prioritizing family, and Rachel apologized for nagging. Their willingness to forgive brought relief and renewed connection.

Biblical Principle: Colossians 3:13 states: *"Bear with one another, and forgive one another, if anyone has a complaint against another; even as Christ forgave you, so you also must do."*

7. Use Godly Mediators if Necessary

Sometimes, conflicts cannot be resolved alone. Couples may need a *trusted mentor, pastor, or counselor* to guide them. God often uses others to provide wisdom, perspective, and accountability.

Example: When Michael and Sarah faced repeated conflicts about extended family boundaries, they invited their pastor for guidance. Through prayer and counseling, they developed clear boundaries, communication strategies, and mutual respect. Their marriage grew stronger because they sought Godly intervention rather than handling it in isolation.

8. Transform Conflict into Growth Opportunities

Conflict is not inherently destructive; it can be *transformative*. Godly wisdom teaches us to extract lessons from disagreement: Learn patience and self-control. Understand your spouse's heart and perspective. Identify personal growth areas. Strengthen emotional intimacy. Improve communication skills

Example: Every disagreement John and Maria faced became an opportunity to *practice humility, prayer, and empathy*. Over time, they noticed fewer arguments and deeper understanding. Their marriage matured because they saw conflict as a stepping stone, not a stumbling block.

9. Daily Practices to Prevent Escalation

Preventing conflicts from becoming destructive requires intentional habits: *Daily prayer together:* Align hearts with God's will. *Regular check-ins:* Discuss issues before they become major conflicts. *Affection and appreciation:* Express love and gratitude consistently. *Clear expectations:* Discuss roles, responsibilities, and priorities.

Example: Every Sunday evening, Lisa and Peter spend 1 hour sharing joys, frustrations, and prayer points. This practice prevents misunderstandings and builds more quickly.

10. Walking in Godly Wisdom

Resolving conflict is not about "winning" or proving a point; it is about *honoring God, respecting your spouse, and preserving unity.* Godly wisdom transforms disputes into opportunities for growth, intimacy, and holiness.

Remember: Pause before responding; Pray for guidance. Speak the truth in love. Listen actively. Forgive freely. Seek Godly counsel when needed.

Conflict, when handled with prayer, humility, and wisdom, becomes a bridge leading couples closer to God and each other.

May your marriage be a reflection of this peace, as you walk together in Godly wisdom and love.

CHAPTER 14

Healing the Unspoken, Overcoming Silent Battles in Marriage

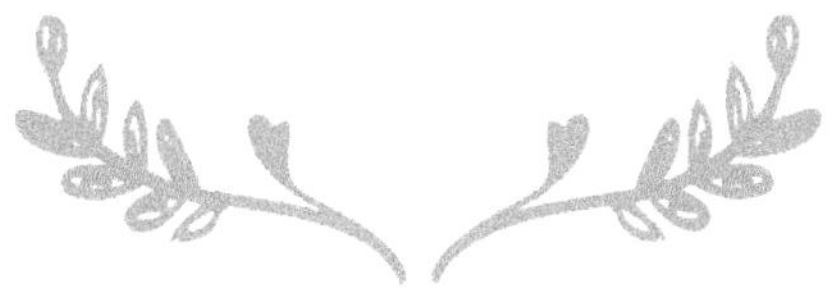

"And be kind to one another, tenderhearted, forgiving one another, even as God in Christ forgave you." Ephesians 4:32

The Hidden Battles

Marriage is meant to be a sanctuary; a place of safety, love, and intimacy. Yet, for many couples, the greatest danger is not loud arguments or dramatic disagreements; it is *the quiet, unspoken battles*; those hurts, frustrations, or disappointments that never find a voice. These silent struggles slowly erode intimacy. They create distance, misunderstandings, and even resentment. Unlike open conflict, which can be addressed, unspoken hurts grow in secrecy.

Consider the story of Sarah and David. They had been married five years, with two young children. On the outside, everything seemed fine. But Sarah felt ignored when David spent evenings watching TV instead of talking to her. David, meanwhile, felt criticized for small household mistakes. Neither voiced their feelings. Over time, frustration built, leading to resentment. Their marriage, once vibrant, became cold and distant, not because of a single argument, but because neither communicated what was in their hearts.

This chapter is about *recognizing, addressing, and healing the unspoken battles* before they destroy the love you share.

1. Why Silent Battles Happen

Silent battles often arise from a combination of pride, fear, and misunderstanding. Many couples avoid speaking about their feelings for several reasons: Fear of conflict, such as *"If I bring it up, we'll fight."* Pride or Ego: "I shouldn't feel this way; it's my spouse who's wrong." Assumptions: "They should know how I feel without me saying it." Past Hurts: Previous experiences make opening up feel unsafe.

When feelings remain bottled up, they manifest in passive-aggressive behavior, withdrawal, or silent resentment. Even small, repeated unspoken issues can feel enormous over time, like a dam holding back a flood.

2. The Cost of Silent Battles

The effects of unspoken hurts are profound: Emotional Distance: Partners feel isolated, lonely, and misunderstood. Lack of Intimacy: Emotional withdrawal often leads to physical and spiritual disconnect. Resentment and Bitterness: Small offenses compound over time into deep-seated anger. Spiritual Weakness: Silent battles allow the enemy to sow division and weaken the unity God intended.

John and Anna had been married for eight years. John quietly resented Anna's long work hours, feeling neglected, while Anna silently resented John for spending too much time with friends. Neither expressed their frustration. Slowly, their home lost warmth. Their friends noticed the tension, but the couple didn't. By the time they sought counseling, the silent battles had been ongoing for years.

3. Signs Your Marriage May Be Facing Silent Battles

It's important to recognize the signs early: Frequent misunderstandings over trivial matters. A sense of walking on eggshells around each other. Feeling emotionally drained or disconnected. Avoiding important conversations to keep the peace. Harboring resentment that never gets addressed. Acknowledging these signs is the first step toward healing. If left unchecked, small misunderstandings can spiral into major marital breakdowns.

4. The Power of Speaking the Unspoken

Communication is the antidote to silent battles. Speaking up doesn't mean fighting; it means sharing feelings with love, honesty, and humility.

Practical steps include: *Start with prayer:* Invite God to guide your words and soften your heart. *Use "I" statements:* Instead of "You never listen," try "I feel unheard when…" *Choose the right time:* Avoid heavy conversations when tired or stressed. *Listen actively:* Truly hear your spouse's heart without preparing a defense.

For example, when Grace finally told her husband about her feelings of neglect, he was initially surprised. But because she expressed herself calmly and lovingly, they were able to work on a weekly *"connection night"* where they spent intentional time together. Their intimacy and trust grew, not overnight, but steadily.

5. Real-Life Examples of Healing Silent Battles

Example 1: Misunderstood Intentions

Mark and Lily often argued about chores. Mark felt Lily didn't appreciate his efforts; Lily felt Mark was overly critical. They never voiced these feelings until a counselor encouraged them to share honestly. Mark learned Lily's critiques were not attacks but attempts to communicate needs. Lily realized Mark needed affirmation for his efforts. The revelation healed years of tension and improved their partnership.

Example 2: Financial Tension

Jenna and Paul avoided talking about money, fearing conflict. Silent anxiety led to secret spending and mistrust. They began weekly financial check-ins, sharing fears and goals openly. This transparency eliminated suspicion and strengthened their bond.

Example 3: Emotional Neglect

Rachel felt unloved when her husband, Tom, worked late every night. Tom felt stressed but didn't realize his absence hurt Rachel. By sharing her emotions without accusation, Tom understood and adjusted his schedule. Rachel felt valued; Tom felt appreciated. A silent battle was transformed into mutual support.

6. Practical Steps to Heal Unspoken Hurts

Identify the Pain: Reflect on what you've been holding back. Journaling can help. *Create Safe Spaces:* Schedule intentional conversations where both partners can speak freely. *Apologize When Needed:* Even small offenses need acknowledgment. A sincere apology brings healing. *Forgive and Release:* Holding onto resentment strengthens silent battles; forgiveness dissolves them. *Pray Together:* Invite God to restore hearts, renew love, and provide wisdom. *Seek Counseling if Necessary:* A neutral third party can help navigate persistent or deep-rooted issues.

7. Prevention: Keeping Communication Healthy

Prevention is better than a cure. Couples can prevent silent battles by: *Checking in daily:* Even five minutes of honest conversation can prevent the accumulation of resentment. *Being emotionally available:* Ask, "How was your day?" and truly listen. *Expressing gratitude:* Celebrate small efforts and affirm your spouse regularly. *Setting boundaries with distractions:* Phones, TV, and social media can create silent disconnects if not managed.

8. The Spiritual Dimension of Silent Battles

Silent battles are not just emotional; they are spiritual. The enemy seeks to divide and discourage couples. By bringing hidden hurts into the light, couples not only heal emotionally but also strengthen their spiritual unity. James 5:16 reminds us: *"Confess your sins to each other and pray for each other so that you may be healed."* While "sins" here often refer to moral failure, the principle applies to hidden offenses, misunderstandings, or emotional neglect. Speaking and praying together brings healing that transforms hearts and homes.

From Silence to Healing

Healing the unspoken is a journey, not a single event. It requires courage, vulnerability, and faith. But the rewards are immeasurable: deeper intimacy, restored trust, and a marriage that mirrors God's love.

What separates strong marriages from struggling ones is the willingness to bring the hidden into the light, address it with love, and walk together toward healing.

Your marriage can be a sanctuary again because you choose covenant love, openness, and forgiveness as your guide.

CHAPTER 15

Maintaining Peace and Joy in the Home

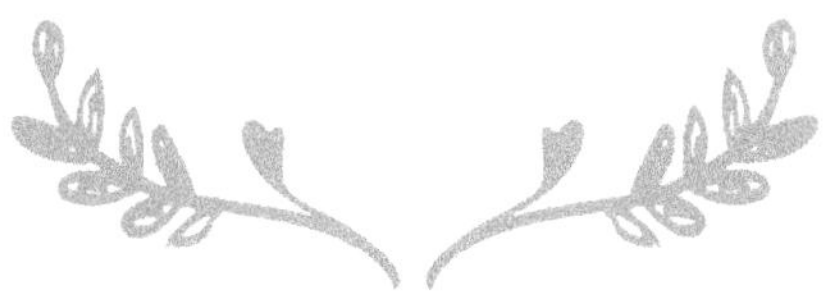

"Better is a dry morsel with quietness, than a house
full of feasting with strife." Proverbs 17:1

A Heavenly Atmosphere at Home

Every marriage longs for a home filled with peace and joy. A house may be beautiful, full of fine furniture and decorated walls, but without peace, it becomes a place of tension and unrest. On the other hand, a small, simple home where peace and joy dwell is truly a *heaven on earth.*

God desires our homes to be sanctuaries of His presence; a place where His Spirit rests, love flows freely, and children feel safe and nurtured. Maintaining peace and joy does not happen by chance; it requires intentional choices, prayerful living, and consistent effort from both husband and wife.

1. Peace: The Foundation of a Godly Home

The Bible teaches us that peace is not merely the absence of conflict but the presence of Christ. Jesus Christ said: *"Peace I leave with you, My peace I give to you; not as the world gives do I give to you. Let not your heart be troubled, neither let it be afraid."* John 14:27

Peace in the home comes when Christ reigns in the hearts of the husband and wife. When both walk in daily fellowship with the Lord, they carry His peace into their home.

Practical steps to cultivate peace:

Begin each day with prayer together, inviting God's Spirit into your marriage. Practice humility, choose reconciliation over winning arguments. Guard against harsh words; choose soft answers (Proverbs 15:1). Keep Christ at the center of decision-making.

Real-life example: James and Mary were constantly arguing about finances. Their home was full of tension. After attending a Bible study, they decided to start praying over their finances together each morning. Slowly, arguments turned into problem-solving conversations. They realized that peace wasn't found in just money, but in *trusting God together.*

2. Joy: The Strength of a Marriage

Nehemiah 8:10 reminds us: *"Do not sorrow, for the joy of the Lord is your strength."* Joy is not dependent on circumstances; it is a fruit of the Spirit (Galatians 5:22). A joyful home is one where laughter is heard, gratitude is expressed, and God's goodness is celebrated daily.

Ways to cultivate joy in the home:

Celebrate small victories: thank God for the little things. *Laugh together often;* joy is a healing medicine (Proverbs 17:22). Share testimonies of God's faithfulness with your spouse and children. Create family traditions that bring lasting memories.

Real-life example: Instead of letting daily stress weigh them down, Samuel and Grace created a family tradition of sharing "one good thing" from the day during dinner. This simple habit shifted the atmosphere from complaining to gratitude, filling their home with joy.

3. The Enemies of Peace and Joy

If peace and joy are so valuable, why do many homes lack them? The Bible identifies several enemies that rob us of peace and joy:

Unforgiveness: Ephesians 4:31–32 urges us to put away bitterness and forgive one another. Anger: James 1:20 reminds us that *"the wrath of man does not produce the righteousness of God."* Fear and Anxiety: Philippians 4:6–7 teaches us to pray instead of worrying. Lack of Gratitude: Complaining creates tension, while thanksgiving brings joy. Couples must identify these enemies and actively resist them through prayer, humility, and love.

4. The Power of Words in the Home

Our words can either build a home filled with peace and joy or tear it down with strife. Speaking harshly or sarcastically may wound deeply, while words of encouragement breathe life.

Practical habits:

Speak blessings over your spouse daily. Replace criticism with constructive words. Read Scripture aloud in the home; it shifts the atmosphere.

Real-life example: David often criticized his wife, Carol, for making small mistakes. She felt discouraged and withdrawn. When David realized the power of his words, he began affirming her strengths instead. Within weeks, Carol blossomed with joy, and their home atmosphere changed dramatically.

5. Building Habits of Peace and Joy

Lasting peace and joy require consistent habits like *Daily Devotions Together*: Reading Scripture and praying builds unity. *Worship at Home*: Playing worship music creates a heavenly atmosphere. *Quality Time*: Regularly invest time in each other without distractions. *Conflict Resolution*: Address disagreements quickly before bitterness grows (Ephesians 4:26).

6. Raising Children in Peace and Joy

Children thrive in homes where peace and joy are present. Colossians 3:21 warns: *"Fathers, do not provoke your children, lest they become discouraged."*

Practical tips for parents: Discipline with love, not anger. Create joyful family moments, game evenings, prayers, and outings. Teach gratitude by modeling thanksgiving to God. Let children see parents reconcile quickly after disagreements. When children witness peace and joy, they grow confident and spiritually strong.

7. Prayer: The Key to Sustaining Peace and Joy

Philippians 4:6–7 gives us the ultimate key: *"Be anxious for nothing, but in everything by prayer and supplication, with thanksgiving, let your requests be made known to God; and the peace of God, which surpasses all understanding, will guard your hearts and minds through Christ Jesus."*

Couples who pray together consistently find it easier to forgive, rejoice, and stay united. Prayer invites God's peace to reign and His joy to overflow in the home.

A Home that Reflects Heaven

A peaceful and joyful home is not free from challenges, but it is one where Christ rules, love abounds, and forgiveness flows. When peace and joy are maintained, the home becomes a testimony to others and a safe place for all who enter.

Remember: Peace comes from Christ's presence. Joy comes from gratitude and fellowship with Him. Both are sustained through prayer, humility, and daily choices. Make your home a sanctuary where heaven touches earth, where peace guards the hearts within, and joy fills every corner.

Couple's Prayer for Peace and Joy

Heavenly Father, we thank You for the gift of our home and for joining us together in covenant love. We ask that Your peace, which surpasses all understanding, guard our hearts and minds through Christ Jesus (Philippians 4:7). Let Your joy be our strength each day, and may our words and actions build an atmosphere of love, laughter, and unity. Teach us to forgive quickly, to speak kindly, and to walk humbly with one another. We invite Your Holy Spirit to dwell richly in our home, making it a sanctuary of Your presence. In Jesus' Name, Amen.

PART IV

Love in Action

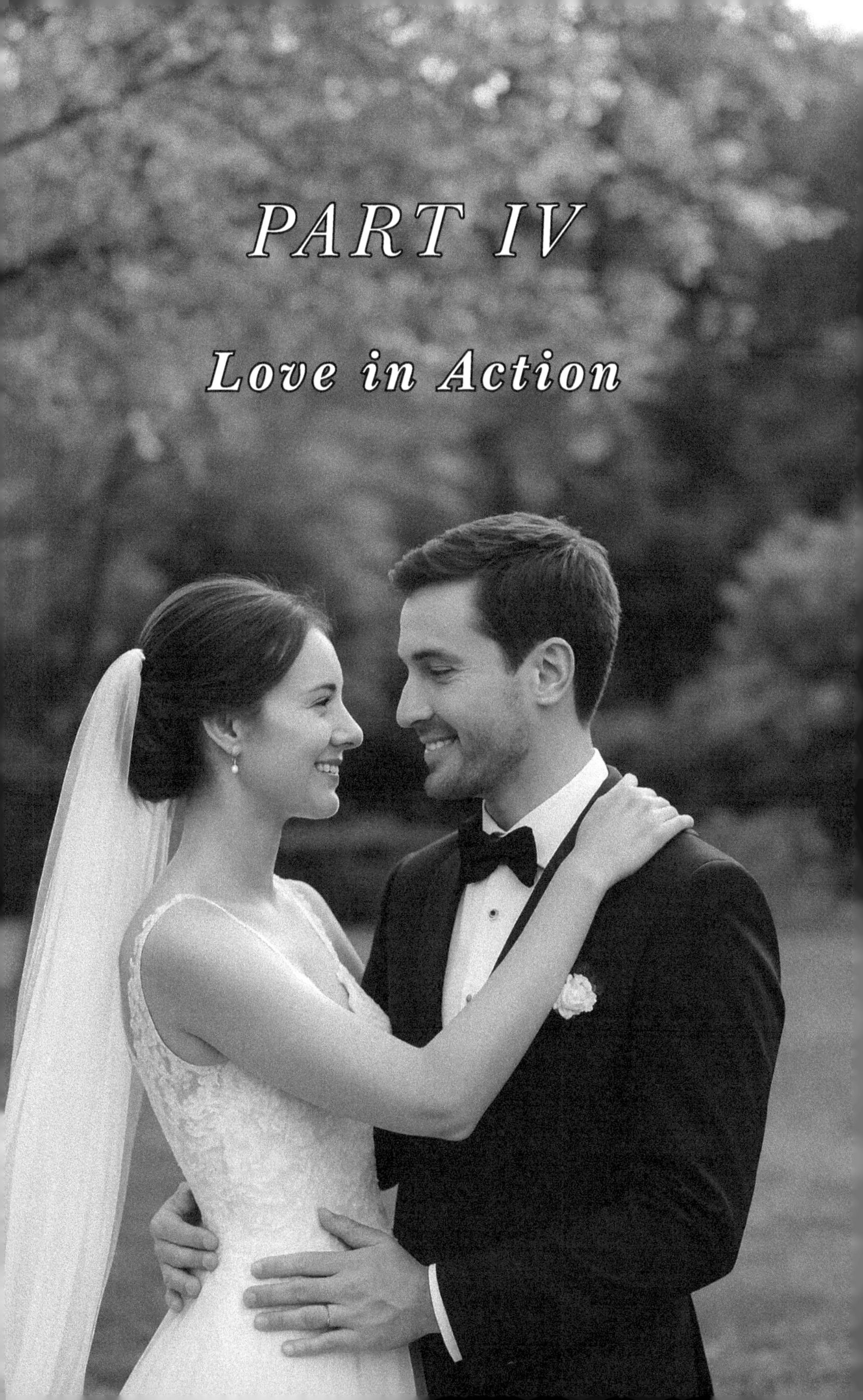

CHAPTER 16

Intentional Romance
In a Busy World

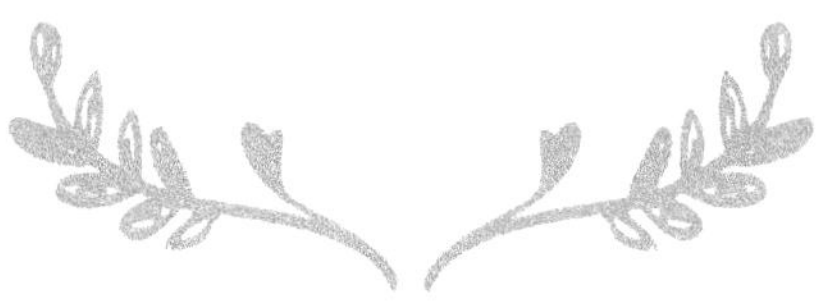

*"And let us consider one another in order to stir
up love and good works." Hebrews 10:24*

Romance That Lasts

Marriage is more than coexisting under one roof; it is a sacred partnership designed for love, intimacy, and joy. Yet, in today's fast-paced world, romance often takes a backseat to work, responsibilities, and daily stress. Husbands and wives may find themselves living like roommates rather than lovers, drifting into routines without nurturing the spark that initially drew them together.

God calls couples to intentional romance, to actively prioritize love, affection, and emotional connection. Romance is not merely about flowers or dates; it is a daily choice to love, honor, and delight in your spouse, no matter how busy life becomes.

1. The Biblical Foundation for Romance

God designed marriage to be intimate, joyful, and filled with love. Song of Solomon celebrates physical, emotional, and spiritual love between a husband and wife: *"Let him kiss me with the kisses of his mouth; For Your love is better than wine."* Song of Solomon 1:2

Romance in marriage is not selfish or worldly; it is God-honoring. When spouses intentionally cultivate love and intimacy, they reflect Christ's love for the Church; faithful, tender, and devoted.

Romans 12:10 reminds us: *"Be kindly affectionate to one another with brotherly love, in honor giving preference to one another."* Intentional romance is rooted in honor, affection, and consistent acts of love.

2. Why Romance Fades in a Busy World

Modern life can steal romance if couples are not vigilant: *Work Pressure*: Long hours, deadlines, and stress leave little energy for emotional connection. *Parenting Demands*: Caring for children is time-consuming and exhausting, often leaving spouses with little personal attention. *Routine and Familiarity*: Daily chores and responsibilities can replace intentional gestures of love. *Distractions*: Technology, social media, and entertainment can become substitutes for a meaningful connection. Without intentionality, romance fades, leaving relationships vulnerable to emotional distance and dissatisfaction.

Example: Mark and Lisa had been married for ten years. Between raising three children and demanding careers, they rarely found time to spend together. Over time, their conversations became practical: about bills, groceries, and school. Their emotional and physical intimacy waned, creating distance that neither noticed until they intentionally set aside time to reconnect.

3. Intentional Romance is a Choice

Romance doesn't happen by accident; it is a deliberate act of love. Couples must *choose to prioritize each other*, even in the midst of life's busyness.

Practical ways to practice intentional romance: Schedule regular date nights; Even simple dinners or walks can renew connection. Leave love notes or messages; Text, emails, or notes expressing appreciation and affection. *Acts of service:* Helping with chores or small tasks shows love in tangible ways. *Physical affection:* Hugs, kisses, and hand-holding reinforce intimacy. *Verbal affirmation:* Compliment, thanks, and verbally express love daily.

Example: Sarah worked long hours and often came home exhausted. Her husband, David, began leaving small notes of encouragement around the house; on the mirror, in her bag, on the fridge. Sarah felt noticed, cherished, and loved, and the small gestures sparked daily conversations and laughter, reminding them of their deep bond.

4. Emotional Intimacy Fuels Romance

Romance is more than physical; it grows from *emotional closeness*. Couples who share their hearts, dreams, and struggles cultivate a deeper connection that strengthens physical and spiritual intimacy.

Daily check-ins: Ask, "How was your day?" and genuinely listen. *Share dreams and goals:* Encourage each other and pray together about personal and family goals. *Celebrate:* Recognize victories, big or small, to reinforce love and appreciation.

Example: John and Emily felt disconnected despite living under the same roof. They started a nightly "pause and talk" ritual; 30 minutes of uninterrupted conversation before bed. Over time, sharing thoughts and dreams daily restored emotional closeness and reignited romance.

5. Romance That Honors God

True romance aligns with God's design. Couples must ensure that their love honors Him, nurtures purity, and brings mutual respect. *Spiritual unity*: Pray together, read the Word, and discuss spiritual insights. *Mutual respect*: Honor each other's boundaries, preferences, and emotional needs. *Faithful love*: Avoid jealousy, mistrust, or distractions that can harm intimacy.

1 Corinthians 13:4–7 reminds us: *"Love suffers long and is kind; love does not envy; love does not parade itself, is not puffed up; does not behave rudely, does not seek its own, is not provoked, thinks no evil; does not rejoice in iniquity, but rejoices in the truth; bears all things, believes all things, hopes all things, endures all things."* When romance is God-centered, it strengthens the marital covenant and reflects His love in practical ways.

6. Overcoming Obstacles to Romance

Even with the best intentions, obstacles could arise: fatigue, stress, disagreements, and life changes can challenge a romantic connection.

Strategies to overcome challenges:

Prioritize connection over perfection: Romance does not require perfect circumstances. *Be creative*: Adapt to your situation: a walk, prayer time, or even a meaningful text can reignite intimacy. *Forgive quickly*: Let go of small offenses that block affection. *Seek help if needed*: Counseling or mentorship can provide tools to restore emotional and physical closeness.

Example: After a tough year filled with stress, Paul and Ruth felt disconnected. They decided to start a "gratitude evening" each Sunday, sharing what they appreciated about each other that week. Even amidst challenges, this intentional time restored their emotional bond and reminded them why they fell in love.

7. Small Daily Gestures Matter

Romance is not only about grand gestures; small, consistent acts create lasting impact:

- Morning hugs or kisses.

- Texts expressing love during the day.

- Holding hands while walking.

- Cooking a favorite meal for each other.

- Sharing a moment of laughter.

These seemingly small acts remind your spouse that they are loved, valued, and cherished, even amid a busy schedule.

8. The Spiritual Dimension of Romance

Romans 12:10 urges: *"Be kindly affectionate to one another with brotherly love, in honor giving preference to one another."* By prioritizing each other, couples reflect God's love. When prayer, worship, and Scripture are part of your daily connection, romance becomes a tool for spiritual unity, blessing both the couple and their household.

Love That Thrives in a Busy World

Intentional romance transforms marriage from routine coexistence into vibrant companionship. By choosing to prioritize your spouse, cultivating emotional intimacy, and honoring God in your love, your marriage becomes a *sanctuary of affection, joy, and spiritual unity*. Romance in marriage is not a luxury; it is a *spiritual discipline*, a daily commitment to nurture love and delight in your spouse, no matter how busy life becomes.

Couple's Prayer for Romance and Intimacy

Heavenly Father, we thank You for the gift of marriage and the love we share. Help us to prioritize each other, to love intentionally, and to cultivate emotional and physical intimacy. Teach us to communicate openly, to forgive quickly, and to honor one another in all things. Fill our hearts with joy, our home with laughter, and our love with Your presence. Let our romance reflect Your perfect love and draw us closer to You and to each other. In Jesus' Name, Amen.

CHAPTER 17

Serving One Another Daily

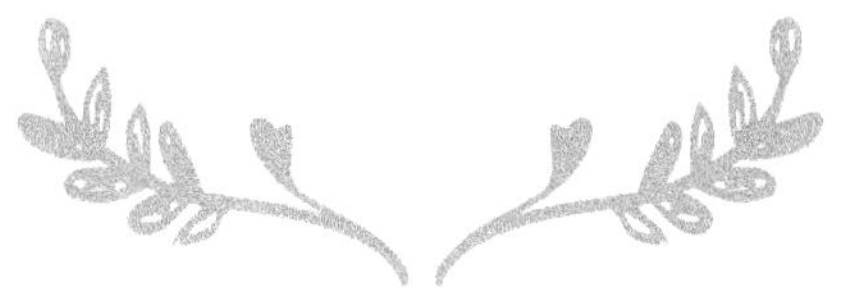

The Heart of True Love

Marriage is not only about receiving love but also about *giving love through service*. True love thrives when both prioritize each other's needs, desires, and well-being. Serving one another daily is an expression of Christlike love that strengthens the marriage bond, deepens trust, and nurtures joy.

In a world that often emphasizes self-interest and personal comfort, intentional acts of service demonstrate *sacrifice, humility, and devotion*. Service is not about obligation; it is a choice to honor, cherish, and uplift your spouse.

1. The Biblical Foundation for Serving Your Spouse

Jesus Christ modeled the ultimate servant heart. John 13:14–15 says: *"If I then, your Lord and Teacher, have washed your feet, you also ought to wash one another's feet. For I have given you an example, that you should do as I have done to you."*

In marriage, serving your spouse is an act of *humility, love, and obedience to God.* Service is not limited to grand gestures; it includes small, daily actions that show care, consideration, and respect.

2. Why Daily Service Matters

Marriage can easily fall into routines where both spouses focus on themselves, unintentionally neglecting each other's emotional, physical, and spiritual needs. Daily service keeps love alive in several ways: *It nurtures intimacy;* Acts of care communicate love and attention. *It builds trust;* Consistent support strengthens confidence in the marriage. *It brings gratitude;* Serving encourages appreciation and mutual respect. *It mirrors Christ's love;* When couples serve selflessly, they reflect God's character.

Example: John noticed his wife, Ruth, was overwhelmed with household tasks after returning from work. Without being asked, he prepared dinner and cleaned up afterward. Ruth felt seen, valued, and loved. These small, intentional acts reminded her daily that their marriage was a union, not a solo journey.

3. Practical Ways to Serve Your Spouse Daily

Service can be simple or elaborate, but consistency is key. Some practical ways include *Acts of kindness;* Making tea, doing laundry, or preparing a meal without being asked. *Listening actively;* Give full attention when your spouse speaks, showing you value their thoughts. *Encouragement;* Speak affirmations, appreciation, and blessings daily. *Support in responsibilities;* Share household chores, parenting duties, and other obligations. *Praying together;* Spiritual service is just as vital as practical help.

Example: Maria often felt unnoticed after long days caring for her children. Her husband, Daniel, began spending ten minutes each morning asking her how he could support her that day. This simple habit made her feel valued, encouraged, and emotionally connected.

4. Serving in Small Gestures Builds Big Love

Sometimes, the smallest acts have the biggest impact. Romance and intimacy grow when service *is frequent, thoughtful, and unselfish.*

- Leaving a loving note on the pillow.

- Bringing coffee in the morning.

- Offering a massage after a long day.

- Doing a chore your spouse dislikes.

These gestures show care without demanding recognition. Matthew 6:3 reminds us: *"But when you do a charitable deed, do not let your left hand know what your right hand is doing."* God blesses marriages where service is humble and sincere.

5. Overcoming Barriers to Serving

Many couples struggle with serving each other consistently due to: *Busyness:* Long work hours or childcare responsibilities. *Pride:* Feeling like "I shouldn't have to do this." *Miscommunication:* Not knowing what the spouse needs.

To overcome these barriers: *Schedule intentional acts of service:* Plan small ways to serve daily or weekly. *Ask and listen:* Communication is essential; find out what your spouse needs. *Cultivate humility:* Serving is an act of love, not weakness. *Pray for a servant heart*: Ask God to give patience, discernment, and willingness.

Example: Peter often expected his wife, Anne, to manage the household without assistance. After a frank conversation, he realized she felt overburdened. He began taking responsibility for cooking twice a week and managing the children's morning routine. This daily service brought peace, joy, and restored harmony in their home.

6. Spiritual Benefits of Serving One Another

Service strengthens more than the emotional bond; it strengthens the spiritual foundation of marriage. Couples who serve each other experience: *Unity in purpose*: Working together cultivates a sense of togetherness. *Mutual growth:* Serving encourages patience, humility, and forgiveness. *A Christ-centered home*: Daily acts of love reflect God's presence in the household.

Galatians 5:13 says: *"For you, brethren, have been called to liberty; only do not use liberty as an opportunity for the flesh, but through love serve one another."* Serving daily is not a duty; it is a lifestyle that demonstrates love through action, inspiring joy, gratitude, and spiritual growth.

7. Real-Life Examples of Service in Marriage

Example 1: Emotional Support: Laura's husband, James, was stressed at work. Instead of ignoring his frustration, Laura took time to pray with him, listen, and offer encouragement. His burdens felt lighter, and their bond grew stronger.

Example 2: Acts of Love in Daily Life: Michael often noticed his wife, Clara, skipping breakfast to get the children ready. He began preparing breakfast for her as an act of love. This small daily gesture transformed her mornings, making her feel cherished and cared for.

8. Making Service a Habit

Consistency is more important than grandeur. Daily service can become a lifestyle through *Intentional planning*; Schedule small acts of service regularly. *Mutual accountability*: Encourage each other to serve consistently. *Reflection and gratitude*: Celebrate each other's efforts, however small. *Prayerful approach*: Ask God to guide your actions and reveal ways to serve. Over time, small acts compound, creating a *marriage marked by love, unity, and joy.*

Love in Action

Serving one another daily is *love in motion.* It is more than tasks; it is a reflection of God's heart, a practical demonstration of care, and a spiritual discipline that strengthens marriage. When both spouses adopt a servant's heart, their home becomes a haven of peace, joy, and intimacy.

The keys are *intentionality, humility, and prayer.* Love grows when it is expressed through consistent, thoughtful actions. As you commit to serving your spouse each day, you will witness your marriage flourishing in ways words cannot describe.

Couple's Prayer for Daily Service

Heavenly Father, we thank You for the gift of our marriage and the opportunity to serve one another in love. Teach us to put each other's needs above our own, to act with humility, patience, and care. Help us recognize opportunities to encourage, support, and bless one another daily. May our acts of service honor You, strengthen our bond, and fill our home with Your peace, joy, and love. In Jesus' Name, Amen.

CHAPTER 18

Raising Godly Children Together

"Train up a child in the way he should go, and when he is old he will not depart from it." Proverbs 22:6

A Sacred Responsibility

Parenting is one of the most important responsibilities in a marriage. Raising children is not simply about meeting their physical needs; it is about nurturing their spiritual, emotional, and moral development. God has entrusted parents with the task of shaping the next generation, and He calls fathers and mothers to partner together in love, guidance, and discipline.

A united approach between husband and wife creates a home where children feel safe, loved, and spiritually secure. Proverbs 1:8 reminds us: *"Hear, my son, your father's instruction, and do not forsake the law of your mother."* Children flourish when they witness harmony, love, and Godly example in their parents' relationship.

1. Parenting as a Team

Children need *both parents actively involved* in their upbringing. When a father and mother serve together, children experience consistency in discipline and values, security in their family environment, and role modeling of teamwork and unity.

Practical strategies for team parenting:

Discuss rules and expectations together before implementing them. Present a unified front in discipline and guidance. Support each other in front of the children, avoid contradicting or undermining one another.

Example: David and Sarah noticed their teenage son was struggling with schoolwork. Instead of addressing him separately, they met together, prayed with him, and created a structured homework schedule. Their united approach gave their son confidence and a sense of security.

2. Leading by Example

Children learn most by observing, not just listening. Husbands and wives must *model Godly character, integrity, and faith. Prayerful life:* Let children see parents praying daily. *Biblical values:* Display honesty, kindness, and patience in your interactions. *Faith in action:* Serve others together as a family. Joshua 24:15 instructs: *"But as for me and my house, we will serve the Lord."* Leading by example instills lasting faith in children. They learn that walking with God is not optional; it is a lifestyle.

Example: Maria and Paul regularly prayed as a family each morning. Their children grew up knowing prayer was a priority, and now, as teenagers, they maintain their own devotional habits.

3. Teaching Biblical Values

Raising Godly children requires intentional teaching. The home is the *primary classroom* for imparting God's Word. Read the Bible together daily. Discuss Scripture in age-appropriate ways. Teach them moral values: honesty, humility, respect, and compassion. Share testimonies of God's faithfulness. Deuteronomy 6:6–7 emphasizes: *"And these words which I command you today shall be in your heart. You shall teach them diligently to your children, and shall talk of them when you sit in your house, when you walk by the way, when you lie down, and when you rise up."*

Example: John and Emily incorporated Bible stories into daily routines. Their children not only memorized Scripture but also applied it in their interactions at school and with friends.

4. Discipline with Love

Discipline is necessary for guiding children, but it must be *loving, consistent, and fair.* Avoid harsh or emotionally charged punishment. Explain the reason for correction. Praise good behavior alongside addressing mistakes. Ephesians 6:4 instructs: *"And you, fathers, do not provoke your children to wrath, but bring them up in the training and admonition of the Lord."* Discipline is most effective when both parents agree and enforce it lovingly.

Example: Tina and Samuel noticed their daughter was lying about homework. Instead of anger, they calmly discussed the consequences and prayed with her about honesty. Their consistent, loving approach led her to confess and take responsibility, strengthening her character.

5. Creating a Spiritually Enriching Environment

A home filled with God's presence makes Godly children. Pray together as a family regularly. *Celebrate spiritual milestones:* baptisms, first memorized verses, acts of service. *Encourage worship* through music, reading, and church participation. *Serve others* as a family to develop compassion and humility.

Psalm 127:3 reminds us: *"Behold, children are a heritage from the Lord, the fruit of the womb is a reward."*

Example: Rachel and Tom made Sunday a special family day, including prayer, worship, and helping a neighbor. Their children grew up associating God with joy, service, and love.

6. Communication: Nurturing Hearts and Minds

Open, honest communication builds trust and emotional security. Encourage children to express feelings freely without fear of judgment, ask questions about God, life, and relationships, and share successes and experiences openly.

Practical tips:

Hold weekly family meetings to discuss challenges and victories. Listen actively without interrupting. Affirm your child's efforts and God-given gifts.

Example: When Samuel noticed his son feeling discouraged about school, he invited him to talk openly about his struggles. Through encouragement and prayer, his son regained confidence and a sense of purpose, and made better grades in school.

7. Balancing Love and Boundaries

Children need love, but they also need boundaries. Boundaries create safety, teach responsibility, and bring respect. Set clear rules and expectations. Follow through consistently. Be flexible but firm when necessary.

Hebrews 12:11 reminds us: *"Now no chastening seems to be joyful for the present, but painful; nevertheless, afterward it yields the peaceable fruit of righteousness to those who have been trained by it."*

Boundaries taught with love cultivate Godliness, discipline, and respect.

Example: Anna and James allowed their children screen time but set limits and discussed appropriate content. The children learned self-control and gratitude, appreciating the balance of freedom and guidance.

8. Praying Together as Parents

Prayer is the backbone of raising Godly children. Parents who pray together model dependence on God and invite His guidance in daily decisions. Pray for wisdom in parenting (James 1:5). Pray for protection over children (Psalm 91:11). Pray for character, faith, and Godly friendships.

Example: Maria and David prayed each night for their children's safety, spiritual growth, and future. Over time, they noticed a deepening faith and moral awareness in their children that mirrored their own devotion.

Raising a Godly Legacy

Raising Godly children is both a privilege and a responsibility. It requires *unity between husband and wife, consistent teaching, loving discipline, spiritual modeling, and prayer.* When parents serve as a team, when they lead by example, and rely on God's guidance, children grow to honor God and reflect His character. Proverbs 20:7 says: *"The righteous man walks in his integrity; his children are blessed after him."* Your marriage sets the foundation for a Godly family. Every prayer, act of service, and moment of guidance leaves a lasting legacy for generations to come.

Couple's Prayer for Raising Godly Children

Heavenly Father, we thank You for the blessing of our children. Teach us to guide them in Your ways with love, patience, and wisdom. Help us to serve one another as parents, to model Godly character, and to nurture our children's hearts and minds. Protect them, strengthen their faith, and make them vessels of Your righteousness. May our home be a sanctuary where Your Word is honored and Your Spirit dwells. In Jesus' name, Amen.

CHAPTER 19

Money, Purpose, and Unity

*"And whatever you do, do it heartily, as to the
Lord and not to men." Colossians 3:23*

Aligning Finances and Purpose in Marriage

Money is one of the most common sources of tension in marriage. When couples fail to communicate or align their financial priorities, even the strongest marriages can experience strain. Yet, money itself is not the enemy. It becomes a tool for blessing, purpose, and partnership when approached with God's wisdom.

Beyond finances, every couple is called to live a *shared purpose,* a vision for life, family, and ministry. Marriage is more than an emotional connection; it is a union where two hearts, two minds, and two callings align under God's plan.

This chapter will guide couples to navigate finances with faith, walk together in purpose, and cultivate true union that reflects God's design.

1. Money: A Tool, Not a Master

Proverbs 21:20 says: *"There is desirable treasure, and oil in the dwelling of the wise, but a foolish man squanders it."* Money in marriage should be *managed wisely*, not feared or idolized. Couples who pray together about finances and make joint decisions find peace and stability.

Practical steps to financial harmony:

Set joint goals: Short-term (groceries, bills), medium-term (vacation, home), and long-term (retirement, children's education). *Budget together*: Transparency prevents suspicion and resentment. *Give generously*: Tithing and charitable giving demonstrate faith and obedience to God. *Avoid debt traps*: Romans 13:8 reminds us, *"Owe no one anything except to love one another."*

Real-life example: Linda and Peter struggled with debt after marriage. Every discussion about money led to arguments. They began to pray together and track every expense in a shared ledger. Gradually, they cleared debts and began saving. Their union strengthened because *they tackled financial challenges together.*

2. Purpose: Discovering God's Plan Together

Ecclesiastes 4:9–10 says: *"Two are better than one, because they have a good reward for their labor. For if they fall, one will lift up his companion. But woe to him who is alone when he falls, for he has no one to help him up."*

Marriage is a union designed to *fulfill God's purpose on earth*. When couples share a vision for life, career, ministry, and family, they move together with clarity and unity.

Practical steps to align purpose:

Pray together about God's calling for your lives. Discuss individual dreams and see where they intersect. Support each other's strengths and gifts. Serve together in ministry, community, or family projects.

Real-life example: Joseph felt called to start a community youth program, while his wife Grace had a heart for mentoring girls. Together, they launched a weekend program for teenage boys and girls. By partnering in purpose, they experienced not only *fruitfulness in ministry* but also a deepening of love and respect in their marriage.

3. Two Become One

Genesis 2:18 reminds us: *"It is not good that man should be alone; I will make him a helper comparable to him."* Marriage is designed as a union. Both husband and wife bring *unique gifts, skills, and perspectives.* True unity is about *mutual respect, shared responsibility, and teamwork,* whether in finances, family decisions, or spiritual growth.

Keys to unity in marriage: Communication: Share dreams, fears, and decisions openly. *Delegation:* Divide responsibilities in a way that complements each other's strengths. *Mutual encouragement:* Celebrate successes and provide comfort during setbacks. *Decision-making together:* From finances to parenting, involve both parties in major choices.

Real-life example: Tina and James had different work schedules. James managed finances, while Tina managed household planning. By recognizing each other's contributions and working as a team, they eliminated conflicts and strengthened their home. Their union became a model of teamwork and trust.

4. Money and Marriage: Avoiding Pitfalls

Mismanagement of money often leads to stress, resentment, and division. The Bible offers timeless guidance: *Avoid greed and materialism:*

1 Timothy 6:10 *"For the love of money is a root of all kinds of evil..."* *Practice contentment*: Hebrews 13:5 *"Let your conduct be without covetousness; be content with such things as you have." Teach financial responsibility to children*: Proverbs 22:6 *"Train up a child in the way he should go, And when he is old he will not depart from it."*

Common pitfalls: Keeping secrets about spending or debt. Prioritizing luxuries over needs or spiritual commitments. Ignoring the other's financial input. Avoiding these pitfalls requires *honesty, prayer, and joint planning.*

5. Purpose and Money Together: Stewardship as a Team

A couple that manages finances with purpose aligns money with God's Kingdom. Every decision becomes an act of worship.

Practical tips: Allocate funds for tithing and charity first. Invest in growth: education, skills, or ministry. Support each other's careers and God-given calling. Pray over financial decisions as a couple.

Real-life example: Faith and Daniel wanted to buy a house. Instead of rushing into debt, they prayed, budgeted, and started a small business together. By combining their skills and resources, they not only bought the house but also created a business that blesses others. Their financial unity became a testimony of faith and God's provision.

6. Spiritual Alignment in Money and Purpose

Colossians 3:23–24 instructs: *"And whatever you do, do it heartily, as to the Lord and not to men, knowing that from the Lord you will receive the reward of the inheritance; for you serve the Lord Christ."*

When couples align finances and purpose under God, they operate in *Kingdom principles,* not just personal ambition. Money becomes a tool for blessing, and purpose becomes a mission to serve God together. Prayer, Bible study, and shared vision keep couples grounded. It prevents selfish ambition, envy, or conflict, replacing them with unity, gratitude, and joy.

7. Maintaining Balance: Work, Home, and Calling

Financial and purpose alignment requires balance. Couples must guard against: Overworking at the expense of marriage, allowing financial stress to dominate the home, and neglecting spiritual growth while pursuing material success.

Practical solutions: Schedule weekly marriage check-ins. Celebrate milestones, no matter how small. Dedicate time for prayer and shared reflection on God's guidance.

Money, Purpose, and Unity

Marriage thrives when money, purpose, and unity are aligned under God. Couples who pray, plan, and serve together experience financial peace, shared vision, and growth. Remember, marriage is *a Divine union*, not just an emotional or practical one. Money is a tool, purpose is a compass, and unity is the foundation. Together, these create a home that reflects God's glory and blesses others.

Couple's Prayer for Money, Purpose, and Unity

Heavenly Father, we thank You for joining us together in covenant love. Teach us to manage our finances wisely, to steward what You have given us for Your glory, and to align our lives with Your divine purpose. Help us walk together as husband and wife, supporting, encouraging, and strengthening one another. May our home reflect Your Kingdom, and may our union bring honor to Your name. In Jesus' name, Amen.

CHAPTER 20

Standing Strong Together

"Though one may be overpowered by another, two can withstand him. And a threefold cord is not quickly broken." Ecclesiastes 4:12

The Strength of Unity

Marriage is designed to be a partnership, a covenant in which two people stand together through life's joys and trials. No matter how strong an individual may be, life's storms can be overwhelming alone. But when husband and wife walk together in unity, they become a fortress against challenges.

Standing strong together is not merely about surviving; it's about thriving, growing stronger spiritually, emotionally, and relationally. It requires teamwork, faith, communication, and reliance on God.

1. Understanding Tribulations in Marriage

Tribulations in marriage can take many forms: Financial struggles, unexpected expenses, or debt. Health challenges. Family and relational conflicts, in-laws, parenting disagreements, or misunderstandings. Spiritual battles, temptation, discouragement, or periods of doubt. James 1:2–4 reminds us: *"My brethren, count it all joy when you fall into various trials, knowing that the testing of your faith produces patience. But let patience have its perfect work, that you may be perfect and complete, lacking nothing."* Tribulations are opportunities for *growth, refinement, and deeper unity* in marriage. Couples who face challenges together develop *resilience, empathy, and spiritual depth.*

Real-life example: Paul and Esther faced a sudden financial crisis when Paul lost his job. Instead of allowing blame or despair to divide them, they prayed together, created a strict budget, and sought God's guidance. The experience strengthened their communication, reliance on God, and commitment to one another. God answered their prayers, they went through that period successfully, and Paul found a better job.

2. Communication: The First Line of Defense

When tribulations come, communication is essential. Silence or withdrawal can lead to misunderstanding, bitterness, and isolation. Proverbs 15:22 says: *"Without counsel, plans go awry, but in the multitude of counselors they are established."*

Practical steps for effective communication:

Be honest but gentle; share fears and struggles without accusing. *Listen actively;* hear your spouse without interrupting or defending. *Affirm your partnership;* remind each other, "We are in this together." *Seek counsel;* mentors, pastors, or counselors can provide Godly guidance.

Real-life example: Linda and Mark were struggling with infertility for two years. Both felt pain and disappointment but had not shared their feelings. A trusted mentor encouraged them to speak openly. Once they began sharing their emotions honestly, they were able to support each other emotionally and spiritually, strengthening their marriage during a difficult season. They continued to pray together, and God gave them beautiful children.

3. Prayer: The Ultimate Source of Strength

Standing strong together requires spiritual unity. Couples who pray together invite God into their homes. Turning fear into faith, and anxiety into peace. Matthew 18:19 promises: *"Again I say to you, that if two of you agree on earth concerning anything that they ask, it will be done for them by My Father in heaven."*

Practical ways to pray together:

Begin each day by committing your marriage to God. Pray specifically for solutions to challenges, not just general blessings. Include prayers of gratitude at all times. Encourage each other to pray individually and corporately.

Real-life example: Joseph and Ruth were experiencing tension over extended family conflicts. They began a nightly prayer routine, praying for wisdom, patience, and unity. Within months, their responses to stressful situations changed; they were calmer, more compassionate, and more united.

4. Mutual Support: Bearing Burdens Together

Galatians 6:2 says: *"Bear one another's burdens, and so fulfill the law of Christ."* Standing strong together means *actively supporting one another emotionally, spiritually, and practically.* Emotionally, listen, comfort, and encourage. Practically, share responsibilities and lighten the load when needed. Spiritually, remind each other of God's promises and walk in faith together.

Real-life example: Sarah's husband, David, was overwhelmed with work and ministry responsibilities. Sarah noticed his stress and took on extra household duties while praying for him daily. David felt supported and encouraged, which strengthened their bond and allowed him to continue his ministry without resentment.

5. Building Unity

Differences don't have to divide; they can actually become opportunities for growth and deeper connection. When both husband and wife choose to listen with empathy, communicate with love, and seek understanding, their relationship becomes stronger and more resilient.

Ephesians 4:26 reminds us, *"Be angry, and do not sin; do not let the sun go down on your wrath."* This verse teaches the importance of resolving issues quickly and with a spirit of peace. Rather than conflict, couples can approach disagreements with grace, patience, and humility, learning more about each other's hearts along the way. When unity is prioritized over pride, love always finds a way to win.

Guidelines for conflict resolution:

Address issues promptly; don't let resentment build. Focus on the problem, not the person. Be willing to apologize and forgive. Seek compromise where possible. Keep God at the center of your resolution process.

Real-life example: Michael and Esther often argued over parenting styles. Instead of escalating, they implemented a weekly "marriage meeting" to discuss issues calmly and make decisions together. Their unity grew, and their children witnessed teamwork and mutual respect.

6. Encouragement and Affirmation

Standing strong together also involves positive reinforcement. Encouragement fuels resilience. Proverbs 16:24 reminds us: *"Pleasant words are like a honeycomb, sweetness to the soul and health to the bones."*

Practical ways to encourage your spouse: Express gratitude daily. Speak affirmations of love and confidence. Celebrate small victories together. Remind each other of God's faithfulness in your marriage.

Real-life example: Rebecca encouraged her husband daily during a season of unemployment, reminding him of his gifts and God's plan. This strengthened his faith and reduced stress, enabling him to find a new job with renewed confidence.

7. Resilience Through Shared Faith

Standing strong together is ultimately about *walking in faith.* Faith gives couples endurance, hope, and perspective. Romans 12:12 says: *"Rejoicing in hope, patient in tribulation, continuing steadfastly in prayer."* Faith creates a shared vision that transcends difficulties. Couples who trust God together remain *steadfast and united,* even when circumstances are challenging.

Practical tips for resilience: Memorize and meditate on encouraging Scriptures together. Keep a *"victory journal"* to record answered prayers. Participate in church or small groups as a couple. Support each other's spiritual growth.

United We Stand

Marriage is not meant to be endured alone. Together, couples can walk with courage, wisdom, and faith. Standing strong together transforms challenges into opportunities for growth, intimacy, and spiritual depth. *Remember:* God equips you as a team. Communication, prayer, and mutual support are keys to resilience. Unity is strengthened through conflict resolution, encouragement, and shared faith. Ecclesiastes 4:12 reminds us: *"A threefold cord is not quickly broken."* Let your marriage be that strong cord, rooted in God, strengthened by unity, and unbreakable in love.

Couple's Prayer for Strength

Heavenly Father, we thank You for joining us together in covenant love. Help us to stand strong together, united in faith, prayer, and love. Teach us to support, encourage, and forgive one another. Let our hearts remain steadfast in You, and may our marriage be a testimony of Your power and grace. In Jesus' name, Amen.

PART V

A Marriage That Reflects Heaven

CHAPTER 21

Marriage and Ministry, Balancing the Call

"But seek first the Kingdom of God and His righteousness, and all these things shall be added to you." Matthew 6:33

A Sacred Balance

Marriage is a holy covenant, and ministry is a divine calling. Both come from God, and both require *commitment, sacrifice, and love.* However, when ministry becomes all-consuming, marriages can suffer. On the other hand, when marriage is not nurtured, the strength of ministry weakens.

God never intended for couples to choose one over the other. Instead, He calls husbands and wives to balance marriage and ministry, serving Him while building a healthy, joyful home. This chapter explores how to walk in unity, honor God's call, and ensure that neither marriage nor ministry is neglected.

1. Marriage as the First Ministry

Before standing behind a pulpit or leading in ministry, every married believer's first calling is to their spouse and family. 1 Timothy 3:5 says: *"For if a man does not know how to rule his own house, how will he take care of the church of God?"* Paul makes it clear: family life is a testimony to spiritual maturity. A minister's effectiveness begins at home. A loving, supportive marriage becomes a platform of credibility and strength in public ministry.

Practical wisdom: Prioritize prayer and devotion as a couple. Make family time non-negotiable. Avoid using ministry as an excuse to neglect your spouse.

Example: Pastor Joseph was passionate about evangelism, but his wife felt abandoned when he was always on the road. After nearly losing their marriage, they began to set boundaries, scheduling evenings together and traveling as a couple whenever possible. Their marriage was restored, and Joseph's ministry became even more fruitful because it was backed by the strength of a united home.

2. Ministry as a Shared Call

Amos 3:3 asks: *"Can two walk together, unless they are agreed?"* God often brings couples together to *complement each other's callings.* While one may preach, the other may intercede, organize, or support behind the scenes. Both roles are vital.

Practical wisdom for shared ministry:

Discover each other's gifts and encourage their use. Avoid competition in ministry; focus on cooperation. Make decisions together about ministry involvement. Respect different levels of calling (one may be more publicly visible while the other serves quietly).

Example: Mary loved teaching children, while her husband David was passionate about worship. Instead of separating their ministries, they created a family-centered service where children learned about God through songs and stories. Their union not only enriched the church but also brought them closer as a couple.

3. Setting Boundaries Between Ministry and Marriage

Ministry can easily consume time, emotions, and energy. Without boundaries, couples risk burnout and neglect of family life. Mark 6:31 records Jesus Christ saying, *"And He said to them, "Come aside by yourselves to a deserted place and rest a while." For there were many coming and going, and they did not even have time to eat."* The Lord Jesus understood the need for rest and balance.

Practical boundaries to establish:

Sabbath rest: Dedicate at least one day to family, free from ministry demands. *Office hours for ministry*: Avoid answering every call at midnight unless it is an emergency. *Family retreats:* Take vacations together for rest and connection. *Private time:* Plan some date nights and quality time for couples.

Example: Rebecca, a pastor's wife, felt isolated because her husband never took breaks. After counseling, they agreed to take Mondays as their "family day." This small boundary transformed their marriage and gave new life to their ministry.

4. Tribulations in Marriage and Ministry

A couple may face challenges, such as financial strain, criticism from church members, or spiritual attacks. How couples respond can either strengthen their union or create division. Ecclesiastes 4:12 says: *"Though one may be overpowered by another, two can withstand him.*

And a threefold cord is not quickly broken." When couples unite in prayer and depend on God, they overcome tribulations together.

Practical responses to challenges:

Never blame each other for ministry struggles. Seek counsel from mature couples in ministry. Fast and pray as a couple when facing opposition. Stand together publicly, even if you need to resolve disagreements privately later.

Example: A pastor and his wife faced false accusations from church members. Instead of fighting each other, they prayed together and remained united. Eventually, the truth came out, and their marriage became a testimony of resilience and faith.

5. Raising a Family in Ministry

One of the greatest challenges is ensuring that children do not feel neglected while parents serve in ministry. Ephesians 6:4 says: *"And you, fathers, do not provoke your children to wrath, but bring them up in the training and admonition of the Lord."* Children must feel loved, valued, and included in the journey of ministry.

Practical steps for families in ministry:

Involve children in age-appropriate ways (ushering, music, helping). Protect family meals and conversations. Listen to their feelings about ministry pressures. Teach them that serving God is a privilege, not a burden.

Example: Pastor Emmanuel always brought his children into ministry activities, but he never pressured them to take roles. They grew up seeing ministry as part of family life, not as a rival for their father's attention. Today, all three serve joyfully in different areas of the church.

6. Unity in Vision: A Couple's Compass

Philippians 2:2 says: *"Fulfill my joy by being like-minded, having the same love, being of one accord, of one mind."* For a couple to balance marriage and ministry, they must be united in vision. Without agreement, bitterness grows. With a shared vision, joy multiplies.

How to maintain unity in vision:

Pray and fast together for ministry direction. Write down family and ministry goals yearly. Revisit and adjust goals together as God leads. Celebrate victories as a team.

7. Practical Keys for Balancing Marriage and Ministry

Prayer and Word Together: Make spiritual intimacy a foundation. *Time Management:* Schedule family, ministry, and rest wisely. *Communication:* Share openly about pressures and needs. *Delegation:* Don't try to do everything yourself; involve others in ministry. *Accountability:* Have mentors or couples to check in with regularly.

A Blessed Balance: Marriage and ministry are not rivals but partners in God's Kingdom. A strong marriage strengthens ministry, and a fruitful ministry blesses marriage. Couples who learn to balance these callings find joy, peace, and lasting impact.

Remember: marriage is a covenant, ministry is a calling, and God is the one who sustains both. When couples walk hand in hand, with Christ at the center, they become unstoppable in love and purpose.

Couple's Prayer for Balancing Marriage and Ministry

Heavenly Father, thank You for calling us both to marriage and to ministry. Teach us to serve You faithfully without neglecting each other. Help us to honor our covenant of love, to manage our time wisely, and to walk in unity of vision. May our marriage be a testimony of Your grace, and may our ministry bear fruit for Your Kingdom. In Jesus' name, Amen.

CHAPTER 22

Your Marriage as a Light to Others

"You are the light of the world. A city that is set on a hill cannot be hidden." Matthew 5:14

Marriage as a Witness

Marriage is not only a private covenant between husband, wife, and God; it is also a *public testimony* of God's love, faithfulness, and design. When couples live in unity, love, and honor, their relationship becomes a *shining light* to their children, extended family, the church, and the world.

When believers allow their marriages to reflect Christ and His Church, they become a *beacon of hope* in a world filled with confusion about love, commitment, and family.

This chapter explores how couples can let their marriage be a light to others through daily living, community impact, and spiritual influence.

1. God's Design: Marriage as a Reflection of Christ

Ephesians 5:31–32 says: *"For this reason a man shall leave his father and mother and be joined to his wife, and the two shall become one flesh. This is a great mystery, but I speak concerning Christ and the Church."*

Marriage is meant to reflect *Christ's relationship with the Church*: a union of sacrificial love, submission, and eternal commitment. When couples love each other in this way, they *preach a silent sermon* to everyone watching.

Practical Application:

The husband shows Christ's love by leading with humility and sacrifice, and the wives reflect the Church by responding with respect and honor. Together, they mirror God's design of unity, not competition.

Example: When neighbors see a couple forgiving each other instead of holding grudges, or speaking with kindness instead of harshness, it plants seeds of curiosity: *"What makes their marriage different?"* That difference is Christ.

2. The Power of Example

1 Peter 2:12 says: *"Having your conduct honorable among the Gentiles, that when they speak against you as evildoers, they may, by your good works which they observe, glorify God in the day of visitation."*

Our marriages are constantly observed by children, church members, coworkers, and friends. We may not even realize how many are watching how we speak, forgive, spend time together, or resolve conflict.

Practical Wisdom:

Show affection publicly but modestly (holding hands, kind words). Resolve disagreements with grace, not shouting. Celebrate milestones: birthdays, anniversaries, and family gatherings. Let children and others witness prayers, not just arguments.

Example: John and Esther always prayed together before meals, even at restaurants. Over time, a coworker noticed and asked them to pray for her family. Their small act of consistency became a light that opened doors for ministry.

3. Hospitality: A Marriage that Welcomes Others

Romans 12:13 says: *"Distributing to the needs of the saints, given to hospitality."* A Godly marriage extends light by opening the home as a place of love, peace, and encouragement. Hospitality allows others to experience the *atmosphere of Christ's presence* within a marriage.

Practical Application:

Host small Bible studies or prayer meetings at home. Invite young couples or singles for meals to observe Godly family life. Use hospitality as discipleship, mentoring others through shared life.

Example: A missionary couple regularly invited students from their church to dinner. These young people often said, *"We've learned more about love and family by being in your home than from any sermon."* Their marriage was preaching louder than words.

4. Marriage as a Witness in Tribulations

It is easy to be joyful when life is smooth, but marriage becomes a true light when couples remain faithful, united, and prayerful during tribulations. Matthew 5:16 reminds us: *"Let your light so shine before men, that they may see your good works and glorify your Father in heaven."*

Practical Application: Stand together in faith when facing opposition from outside. Support each other through financial hardship with prayer and teamwork. Show forgiveness publicly when offenses arise.

5. Parenting as a Testimony

Children often become the greatest reflection of a marriage. How parents raise their children demonstrates the health of their covenant. Proverbs 22:6 says: *"Train up a child in the way he should go, and when he is old he will not depart from it."*

Practical Wisdom: Model forgiveness, not bitterness, before children. Prioritize family devotion time. Teach children respect by how spouses treat each other. Share responsibilities so children see teamwork, not division.

Example: David and Ruth prayed with their children every night. Their consistent example inspired one of their teenage neighbors, who asked to join. Years later, that neighbor testified, *"It was seeing their family pray that led me to Christ."*

6. Guarding Against Hypocrisy

The greatest danger to being a light is living one way in public and another in private. Hypocrisy dims the witness of marriage. Titus 2:7–8 says: *"In all things showing yourself to be a pattern of good works; in doctrine showing integrity, reverence, incorruptibility, sound speech that cannot be condemned..."*

Practical Guardrails: Be the same person at home and in church. Resolve conflicts privately before ministering publicly.

Example: A church leader constantly spoke about love but was rude to his wife in public. Many young people in the church turned away, saying, *"If that is what Christian marriage looks like, we don't want it."* His hypocrisy harmed his witness.

7. Marriage as Evangelism

A Godly marriage often preaches louder than sermons. People who would never step into a church may be drawn to Christ because of the peace, joy, and love they see in a couple's relationship. 1 Corinthians 13:4-7 describes love as: *"Love suffers long and is kind; love does not envy; love does not parade itself, is not puffed up; does not behave rudely, does not seek its own, is not provoked, thinks no evil; does not rejoice in iniquity, but rejoices in the truth; bears all things, believes all things, hopes all things, endures all things."* When couples live out this love, they show the world what God's love looks like.

Practical Application: Invite unbelieving friends into your home. Share your testimony of how Christ sustains your marriage. Live consistently so others ask about your faith.

8. The Reward of Being a Light

Philippians 2:15 says: *"…that you may become blameless and harmless, children of God without fault in the midst of a crooked and perverse generation, among whom you shine as lights in the world."*

When couples let their marriage shine, their children inherit a Godly legacy, their church is strengthened by their example, and their community sees Christ through them. Heaven rejoices as souls are drawn to God.

A Marriage That Glorifies God

Marriage is more than a private journey; it is a divine assignment to reflect God's love on earth. Couples who embrace this calling will inspire others, disciple younger believers, and demonstrate to unbelievers the transforming power of Christ. When your marriage is filled with love, forgiveness, and joy, you are not just living for yourselves; you are lighting the path for others to find God.

Couple's Prayer for Being a Light

Heavenly Father, thank You for our marriage and the covenant we share. Help us to be a reflection of Your love to our children, church, and community. Teach us to walk in unity, forgiveness, and joy, so that others may see Christ in us. May our home be a testimony that draws people to You. In Jesus' name, Amen.

CHAPTER 23

Guarding Your Marriage in a Broken World

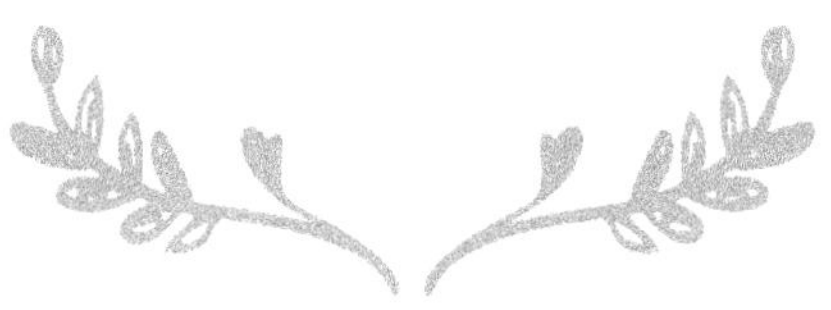

"Watch, stand fast in the faith, be brave, be strong." 1 Corinthians 16:13

A Call to Spiritual Vigilance

We live in a world where marriage is constantly under attack. The culture normalizes divorce, celebrates immorality, and undermines covenant love. The media glorifies lust, self-gratification, and temporary relationships. Even within the church, many marriages struggle under pressure from temptation, stress, and busyness.

In such a broken world, Christian couples must make a *deliberate decision to guard their marriage.* A thriving, Christ-centered marriage will not happen by chance; it requires *vigilance, prayer, discipline, and love.*

This chapter explores *biblical principles, practical steps, and spiritual wisdom* for safeguarding your marriage against the forces that seek to destroy it.

1. Recognize the Enemy's Strategy Against Marriage

John 10:10 reminds us: *"The thief does not come except to steal, and to kill, and to destroy. I have come that they may have life, and that they may have it more abundantly."* The enemy knows that when marriages are strong, families flourish, and the church grows. That is why he targets marriages with division, temptation, and confusion.

Common attacks on marriage in today's world:

Temptation through lust and pornography: Emotional affairs via social media connections, financial pressures causing stress and arguments, overwork and busyness leading to neglect of intimacy, and Cultural messages that devalue faithfulness and covenant.

Practical wisdom: Guard your marriage by acknowledging that *you are in a spiritual battle.* Put on the whole armor of God daily (Ephesians 6:10–18).

2. Guarding the Heart and Mind

Proverbs 4:23 says: *"Keep your heart with all diligence, for out of it spring the issues of life."* The battle for your marriage begins in the heart and the mind. What you entertain in your thought life will eventually shape your actions.

Practical ways to guard your heart: Be mindful of what you watch, read, or listen to. Avoid flirting or entertaining impure thoughts. Speak affirming words about your spouse rather than comparing them with others. Build a habit of gratitude for your partner.

Example: Anna once struggled with comparing her husband to a colleague at work. When she recognized the danger, she began intentionally thanking God for her husband's unique qualities. Her perspective shifted, and her marriage grew stronger.

3. Protecting Intimacy in Marriage

Hebrews 13:4 says: *"Marriage is honorable among all, and the bed undefiled; but fornicators and adulterers God will judge."* In a broken world filled with sexual immorality, couples must intentionally protect their intimacy. Intimacy is more than physical; it includes *emotional, spiritual, and relational closeness.*

Practical steps to protect intimacy: Make time for regular date nights. Communicate openly about needs and desires. Do not let unresolved conflicts linger; deal with them quickly (Ephesians 4:26). Avoid secretiveness in communication, devices, or finances. Pray together.

Example: One couple noticed they were drifting apart emotionally because of busy schedules. They decided to pray together every night, even if only for ten minutes. This simple act rekindled both spiritual and emotional closeness.

4. Guarding Against the Influence of the World

Romans 12:2 says: *"And do not be conformed to this world, but be transformed by the renewing of your mind..."* The world normalizes infidelity, cohabitation without commitment, and treating marriage as disposable. If couples are not careful, these cultural messages can subtly influence their expectations and attitudes.

Practical ways to resist worldly influence: Be selective with entertainment, avoid shows or music that glorify adultery or lust. Surround yourselves with Godly couples and mentors who inspire you. Raise your children with biblical values of purity, faithfulness, and respect. Choose community over isolation, belong to a church family that strengthens marriages.

5. Financial Integrity and Contentment

Many marriages are destroyed not by infidelity but by financial conflict. The world pressures couples to chase materialism, often at the expense of unity. 1 Timothy 6:6 reminds us: *"Now Godliness with contentment is great gain."*

Practical steps for financial guarding: Create a budget together and stick to it. Avoid secret spending or hidden debts. Make financial decisions in unity. Be content with what God has provided while working diligently.

Example: Daniel wanted to buy a new car, but his wife felt it was not wise financially. Instead of arguing, they prayed about it and delayed the purchase. Months later, an unexpected expense arose, and they were thankful they had waited.

6. The Role of Prayer and the Word

Psalm 127:1 declares: *"Unless the Lord builds the house, they labor in vain who build it."* Guarding your marriage is possible with God. Prayer and the Word of God are the greatest defenses against the brokenness of the world.

Practical prayer practices for couples: Pray together daily, even briefly. Declare Scripture over your marriage (e.g., 1 Corinthians 13:4–7). Fast together during seasons of challenge. Keep a family altar; a time set apart for worship and Bible reading.

7. Accountability and Transparency

James 5:16 says: *"Confess your trespasses to one another, and pray for one another, that you may be healed."* Openness and honesty are vital. Secrecy weakens trust, while transparency builds security.

Practical applications: Share passwords and avoid secret online interactions. Be accountable to a mentor couple or pastor. Talk about struggles rather than hiding them. Be quick to repent and forgive when mistakes happen.

8. Teaching the Next Generation

Deuteronomy 6:6–7 says: *"And these words which I command you today shall be in your heart. You shall teach them diligently to your children…"* Guarding your marriage also means passing down Godly values to your children. In a broken world, kids are exposed early to distorted views of relationships. A healthy marriage becomes a *living testimony* that shapes their future choices.

Practical ways to teach children: Model respect and love in front of them. Teach them about purity and Godly dating. Let them see you resolve conflicts peacefully. Pray for their future marriages.

A Marriage Built to Last

Guarding your marriage in a broken world requires vigilance, prayer, and intentionality. The enemy does not stop attacking, but with Christ at the center, your marriage can thrive and become a light in the darkness.

Remember: you are not fighting alone. The Spirit of God equips you; the Word strengthens you, and the grace of Jesus Christ sustains you. A Christ-centered marriage will not only survive the brokenness of the world but will shine as a testimony of hope.

Couple's Prayer for Guarding Our Marriage

Lord Jesus, we thank You for the gift of marriage. We recognize that we live in a world filled with temptation, distraction, and brokenness. Today, we ask for Your protection over our hearts, our minds, our home, and our family. Help us to stay faithful, united, and strong in You. Teach us to guard our love with wisdom and prayer. May our marriage reflect Your covenant love and bring glory to Your name. In Jesus' name, Amen.

Build on the Right Foundation

Jesus Christ said in Matthew 7:24–27: *"Therefore whoever hears these sayings of Mine, and does them, I will liken him to a wise man who built his house on the rock: and the rain descended, the floods came, and the winds blew and beat on that house; and it did not fall, for it was founded on the rock.*

But everyone who hears these sayings of Mine, and does not do them, will be like a foolish man who built his house on the sand: and the rain descended, the floods came, and the winds blew and beat on that house; and it fell. And great was its fall."

Here, Jesus Christ compares two builders. Both faced the same storms: the rain, the floods, the wind, but their outcomes were different. One house stood firm, and the other fell. The difference was the *foundation*. The wise builder built on the rock; the foolish man built on sand.

In marriage, external challenges, financial hardship, social pressures, family interference, or even social media advice can act like storms. Some social media platforms teach women to manipulate or control their husbands, while others encourage men to misbehave in marriage. If couples follow these sources rather than God, their marriages are vulnerable.

Obedience to God is essential: *"Therefore whoever hears these sayings of Mine, and does them..."* When couples choose to follow God's principles for marriage rather than relying solely on emotions or personal preferences, they lay a solid foundation that can withstand any storm. God's Word provides the wisdom and stability every marriage needs to flourish and stand firm. Marriage is governed by principles and laws, much like society.

"Build your house on the rock, and it shall stand."

Proverbs 24:3–4 teaches us: *"Through wisdom a house is built, and by understanding it is established; by knowledge the rooms are filled with all precious and pleasant riches."*

Information is the starting point. You cannot reach wisdom without knowledge. *Understanding* comes from digesting knowledge through life experiences and testing it in real situations. *Wisdom* emerges when knowledge and understanding transform into action and discernment.

Marriage Requires Knowledge, Understanding, and Application

A family can prosper across generations, creating wealth and raising Godly children, but it requires deliberate effort. Just as talents must be nurtured through training, discipline, and knowledge, blessings also require this same nurturing. Wealth, natural resources, or even beauty alone are not enough to sustain a marriage.

The Spiritual and Moral Foundation

Marriage is more than emotions or convenience; it is a **covenant**. The spiritual and moral qualities of both spouses determine the strength of the marriage: both must be born-again believers, walking in holiness and integrity. Spiritual maturity and discipleship shape behavior, speech, and decision-making in marriage. Obedience to God's Word is non-negotiable. Proverbs 24:6 reminds us: *"For by wise counsel you will wage your own war, and in a multitude of counselors there is safety."*

Building a Marriage: A Strategic Model

Think of a marriage as a **house**:

Many focus only on the roof, how to "manage" the relationship, while ignoring the foundation. The foundation shapes everything: obedience to God, covenant understanding, character, and spiritual maturity. Without it, no amount of gifts, wealth, or trips abroad can make a marriage sustainable.

Marriage as a House

Roof (20%) Relationship Management: Represents love, communication, trust, conflict resolution, and how the couple manages day-to-day issues.

Walls (30%) Knowledge & Word of God: Biblical principles, wisdom, understanding of each other, learning, and growth keep the house strong.

Foundation (40%) Spirituality & Morality of the 2 People: The deepest layer: faith in God, values, integrity, and spiritual alignment. Without this, the house cannot stand.

Environment (10%) External Factors: Family background, friends, culture, finances, society. These influence the house very little; they are not the core.

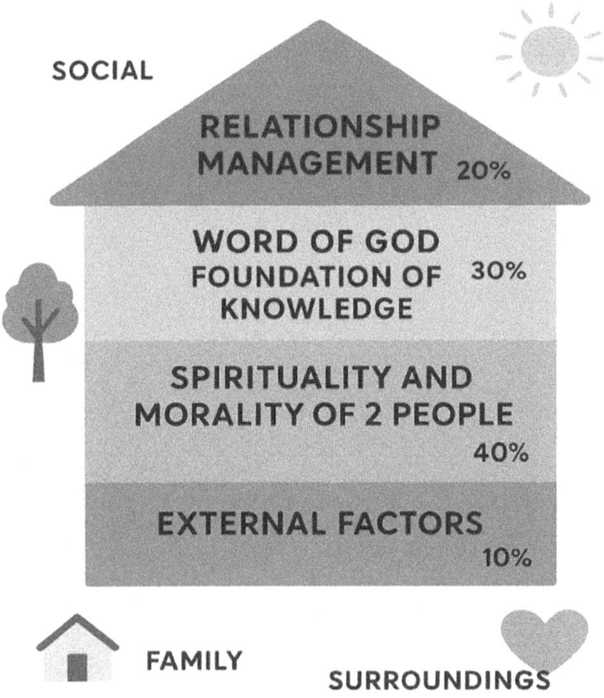

Avoiding Distractions and Deception

Today, society and media often promote superficial measures of success in marriage: Expensive dinners, lavish gifts, vacations, or luxury items. Social media influencers may claim happiness comes from wealth or external appearances. But true marital success is built on a spiritual foundation, moral integrity, and mutual submission to God's Word. Marriage is a divine union designed to glorify God, strengthen families, and secure your destiny. Guard it, build it wisely, and never let the enemy steal what God has entrusted to you.

CHAPTER 24

A Home Filled With Gratitude and Worship

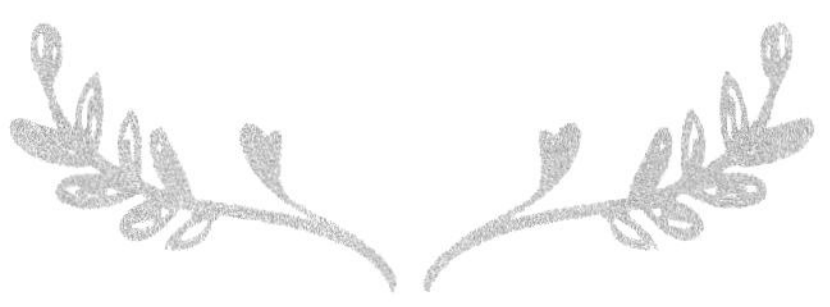

Building the Right Atmosphere in the Home

Every home carries an *atmosphere.* Some homes are filled with tension, fear, or constant complaining. Others radiate peace, love, and joy. What makes the difference? It is not wealth, comfort, or possessions, but the **spiritual culture cultivated** inside the home.

When gratitude and worship become the foundation of a family, the home shifts from being a place of survival to a dwelling place of God's presence. A grateful and worshipping home becomes a *sanctuary of strength,* where faith grows, relationships deepen, and God's blessings are multiplied.

This chapter will show why gratitude and worship are powerful forces for your marriage and family, and how to intentionally cultivate them in your home.

1. Gratitude: The Key to Unlocking Joy in the Home

Philippians 4:6–7 declares: *"Be anxious for nothing, but in everything by prayer and supplication, with thanksgiving, let your requests be made known to God; and the peace of God, which surpasses all understanding, will guard your hearts and minds through Christ Jesus."*

Gratitude is not just polite manners; it is a *spiritual discipline* that shifts the atmosphere of a home. A complaining spirit repels peace, but a grateful heart invites God's presence.

Benefits of gratitude in marriage and family life:

Builds contentment and reduces comparison. Strengthens bonds between spouses and children. Turns ordinary moments into Worship. Guards against bitterness and entitlement.

Practical habits of gratitude in the home:

Speak daily words of appreciation to your spouse. Teach children to thank God for small things. Keep a "family gratitude journal" where everyone records blessings. End each day by sharing three things you are thankful for.

Example: A family in crisis began a nightly practice of thanking God for three blessings each. Slowly, their perspective shifted, and peace returned to their home.

2. Worship: Making Your Home a Dwelling Place for God

Psalm 22:3 says: *"But You are Holy, enthroned in the praises of Israel."* God dwells where He is worshipped. When a home is filled with worship, His presence brings *healing, joy, and deliverance.* Worship transforms an ordinary house into a *house of God's Glory.*

Practical expressions of worship at home:

Start mornings with worship music and prayer. Sing hymns or worship songs together as a family. Dedicate a "family altar" time for Scripture and praise. Let worship flow naturally while cooking, cleaning, or driving.

Why worship matters in marriage:

Worship unites couples in the Spirit. Helps shift focus from problems to God's Greatness. Invites divine wisdom and guidance.

3. Gratitude and Worship as Weapons Against Darkness

Colossians 3:15–16 exhorts us: *"And let the peace of God rule in your hearts, to which also you were called in one body; and be thankful. Let the word of Christ dwell in you richly… singing with grace in your hearts to the Lord."*

We live in a broken world, where fear, anxiety, and negativity bombard families daily. Gratitude and worship are not just attitudes; they are *weapons of spiritual warfare.* Gratitude destroys the spirit of discontent and envy. Worship pushes back oppression and ushers in God's light. Together, they silence the enemy's lies with God's truth.

Example: A couple struggling with depression began each morning with worship songs. Over time, the heavy atmosphere lifted, replaced with joy and renewed faith.

4. Teaching Gratitude and Worship to Children

Proverbs 22:6 says: *"Train up a child in the way he should go, and when he is old he will not depart from it."* Children naturally absorb the culture of their home. If complaining dominates the household, they will carry it into adulthood. But if gratitude and worship define the environment, they will grow up with a heart that seeks God.

Practical ways to teach children:

Lead by example; let them hear you thanking God and others often. Teach them simple worship songs and memory verses. Involve them in family prayer times. Celebrate answered prayers together.

5. Healing Relationships Through Gratitude and Worship

Colossians 3:17 says: *"And whatever you do in word or deed, do all in the name of the Lord Jesus, giving thanks to God the Father through Him."* Many marriages suffer from silent resentment or constant criticism. Gratitude and worship can heal wounds by changing how couples see each other. Gratitude replaces criticism with appreciation. Worship reminds couples of their unity in Christ. Together, they renew love and restore intimacy.

Example: A husband who rarely thanked his wife started affirming her daily. Within weeks, her sense of worth in the marriage grew, and their love deepened.

6. Creating a Culture of Thanksgiving and Worship

Joshua 24:15 declares: *"But as for me and my house, we will serve the Lord."* A grateful and worshipping home does not come by accident; it is built by *consistent habits and deliberate choices.*

Steps to create this culture:

Set rhythms: Morning devotion, evening gratitude circle. *Use music intentionally:* Play worship songs instead of worldly entertainment. *Celebrate milestones with thanksgiving:* Birthdays, anniversaries, promotions. *Pray blessings over family members aloud.* Over time, these small actions cultivate an atmosphere where God's presence fills the home.

7. The Overflow of a Worshipping Home

Psalm 100:4 says: *"Enter into His gates with thanksgiving, and into His courts with praise. Be thankful to Him, and bless His name."*

A grateful and worshipping home becomes a beacon to others. Guests who enter will feel peace. Children raised there will carry the atmosphere into their own homes. The marriage itself becomes a witness to God's faithfulness.

Blessings of a worshipping home:

Increased joy and peace.

Stronger unity in marriage.

Children grounded in faith.

A testimony that draws others to Christ.

Building a Sanctuary at Home

In a world filled with negativity, fear, and brokenness, a grateful and worshipping home shines as a sanctuary of light. Such a home is not defined by wealth or perfection but by hearts surrendered to God.

When spouses commit to daily gratitude and worship, their love grows deeper, their faith becomes stronger, and their family becomes a living testimony of God's presence.

Family Prayer for Gratitude and Worship

Father, we thank You for the gift of our home. We ask that You fill our home with Your peace, joy, and presence. Teach us to live with grateful hearts, always remembering Your goodness. Help us to worship You not only with our lips but with our lives. May our marriage and family be a dwelling place of Your Spirit, shining as a light in this world. We dedicate our home to You, in Jesus' name. Amen.

CHAPTER 25

Growing Old together in God's Love

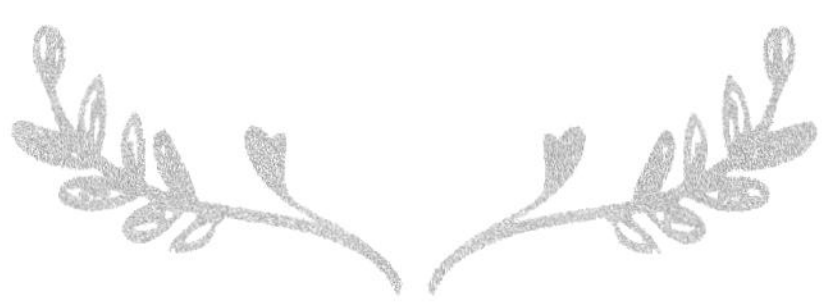

*"Even to your old age, I am He, and even to gray hairs
I will carry you! I have made, and I will bear; even I
will carry, and will deliver you." Isaiah 46:4*

Love That Endures the Seasons

Every marriage begins with the joy of new love, the excitement of discovery, passion, and shared dreams. But the true beauty of marriage is not found in its beginnings; it is revealed in its endurance and faithfulness over time.

In a world that celebrates youth and novelty, God calls Christian couples to embrace the beauty of growing old together in His love. Aging is not something to fear; it is a testimony of God's grace and faithfulness. The wrinkles, gray hairs, and slowing steps tell a story of love preserved by the Lord.

This chapter will explore what it means to age gracefully in marriage, keeping God at the center, nurturing intimacy, and leaving a legacy of love.

1. God's Promise to the Aging Couple

Isaiah 46:4 assures us: *"Even to your old age, I am He, and even to gray hairs I will carry you! I have made, and I will bear; even I will carry, and will deliver you."*

God does not abandon His children in their old years. He promises to sustain, carry, and deliver us. This includes sustaining marriages.

As couples grow older, physical strength may decline, but spiritual strength increases when rooted in Christ. The love of God becomes the foundation that holds two hearts together when everything else changes.

Practical reflection: Instead of fearing aging, couples can look forward to it as a season of deeper companionship and closer dependence on God.

2. Embracing Change Together

Ecclesiastes 3:1 reminds us: *"To everything there is a season, a time for every purpose under heaven."* Every stage of marriage brings change: raising children, financial adjustments, career shifts, and eventually retirement. Some couples resist change but embracing it together with faith strengthens love.

Practical wisdom for embracing change:

Communicate openly about new needs and limitations. *Support* each other's physical, emotional, and spiritual transitions. *Learn* new ways of showing love; what worked at age 30 may differ at age 70. *Celebrate* milestones, anniversaries, and all victories together.

3. Growing Deeper in Intimacy

Song of Solomon 8:7 says: *"Many waters cannot quench love, nor can the floods drown it."* As years pass, physical attraction may fade, but *true intimacy deepens.* Growing old together allows couples to know each other's thoughts, habits, and dreams in a way no one else can.

Practical steps for deepening intimacy in old age:

Keep pursuing each other through thoughtful gestures. Maintain physical affection; a gentle touch, hug, or kiss communicates love. Share spiritual intimacy by reading Scripture and praying together. Talk about memories, recount God's faithfulness.

Reflection: In old age, intimacy becomes less about passion and more about union, care, and spiritual oneness.

Growing old in God's love is not a decline but a *fulfillment of His promises.* As couples walk hand in hand through the seasons of life, their love becomes a testimony of Christ's covenant with His Church.

God honors marriages that endure through decades. A Christ-centered marriage grows more beautiful with age, becoming a beacon of faith for children, grandchildren, great-grandchildren, and the church.

Couple's Prayer for Growing Old in God's Love

Heavenly Father, we thank You for the gift of life and the blessing of walking together in marriage. As we grow older, help us to grow deeper in love for You and for one another. Teach us to embrace every season with joy and faith. May our marriage reflect Your covenant of love forever. In Jesus' name, Amen.

Appendices

(A)
31-Day Prayer Guide
for Couples

"Again I say to you that if two of you agree on earth concerning anything that they ask, it will be done for them by My Father in heaven." Matthew 18:19

Why Pray Together?

Prayer is the lifeline of every Christian marriage. It is where couples invite God into their relationship, seek His wisdom, and surrender their burdens at His feet. A marriage that prays together grows stronger in unity, intimacy, and resilience.

This *31-Day Prayer Guide* is designed to help couples pray consistently for one another and for their marriage. Each day has a Scripture, a focus theme, and a short model prayer that can be prayed together.

31 Days of Prayer for Couples

Day 1: Foundation in Christ

"For no other foundation can anyone lay than that which is laid, which is Jesus Christ." 1 Corinthians 3:11

Prayer: Lord Jesus, You are the foundation of our marriage. Help us to build every part of our lives on You, that our love may stand firm in every season.

Day 2: Love That Endures

"Love suffers long and is kind…" 1 Corinthians 13:4

Prayer: Father, teach us to love each other with patience and kindness. Let our love reflect Your unconditional love.

Day 3: Unity in Spirit

"Endeavoring to keep the unity of the Spirit in the bond of peace." Ephesians 4:3

Prayer: Lord, make us one in heart and mind. Help us walk in agreement and maintain peace in our home.

Day 4: Forgiveness

"And be kind to one another, tenderhearted, forgiving one another, even as God in Christ forgave you." Ephesians 4:32

Prayer: Father Lord, give us hearts quick to forgive. Let no bitterness take root in our marriage.

Day 5: Protection from Temptation

"And do not lead us into temptation, but deliver us from the evil one." Matthew 6:13

Prayer: Lord, shield us from the schemes of the enemy. Keep our hearts pure and faithful to one another.

Day 6: Joy in the Home

"The joy of the Lord is your strength." Nehemiah 8:10

Prayer: Lord, fill our home with laughter, happiness, and joy that comes from You alone.

Day 7: Wisdom for Decisions

"If any of you lacks wisdom, let him ask of God…" James 1:5

Prayer: Father, guide us in every decision we make as a couple. Let Your wisdom lead our steps in Jesus' Mighty name.

Day 8: Financial Stewardship

"Moreover it is required in stewards that one be found faithful." 1 Corinthians 4:2

Prayer: Lord, help us manage our finances wisely, giving generously and living faithfully.

Day 9: Health and Strength

"But those who wait on the Lord
Shall renew their strength;
They shall mount up with wings like eagles,
They shall run and not be weary,
They shall walk and not faint. Isaiah 40:31

Prayer: Father, bless us with health and strength to serve You and each other faithfully.

Day 10: Intimacy and Affection

"Let the husband render to his wife the affection due her, and likewise also the wife to her husband." 1 Corinthians 7:3

Prayer: Lord, help us nurture intimacy and affection in our marriage, reflecting Christ's love for His Church.

Day 11: Parenting with Grace

"Train up a child in the way he should go,

And when he is old he will not depart from it." Proverbs 22:6

Prayer: Father, give us wisdom to raise our children in Your ways and lead them by example.

Day 12: Serving Together

"As for me and my house, we will serve the Lord." Joshua 24:15

Prayer: Lord, use us as a family to serve You and others with glad hearts.

Day 13: Peace in Conflict

"Blessed are the peacemakers, for they shall be called sons of God." Matthew 5:9

Prayer: Father, help us resolve conflicts quickly and peacefully, with humility and love.

Day 14: Patience in Trials

"But let patience have its perfect work, that you may be perfect and complete, lacking nothing." James 1:4

Prayer: Lord, if trials come, help us stand together with faith and patience, trusting in You.

Day 15: Gratitude

"In everything give thanks; for this is the will of God in Christ Jesus for you." 1 Thessalonians 5:18

Prayer: Father, teach us to be grateful for one another and for every blessing in our marriage in Jesus' Precious name.

Day 16: Friendship in Marriage

"A friend loves at all times…" Proverbs 17:17

Prayer: Lord, make us best friends as well as husband and wife. May we enjoy each other's company daily.

Day 17: Faith to Overcome

"For we walk by faith, not by sight." 2 Corinthians 5:7

Prayer: Lord, strengthen and deepen our faith so we can rise and grow together with confidence and joy.

Day 18: Guarding Purity

"Blessed are the pure in heart, for they shall see God." Matthew 5:8

Prayer: Father, guard our hearts, eyes, and minds. Keep us faithful in thought and deed.

Day 19: Hope for the Future

"For I know the thoughts that I think toward you, says The Lord, thoughts of peace and not of evil, to give you a future and a hope." Jeremiah 29:11

Prayer: Lord, fill us with hope for the future You have prepared for us as a couple.

Day 20: Humility in Love

"With all lowliness and gentleness, with longsuffering, bearing with one another in love." Ephesians 4:2

Prayer: Father, help us walk in humility and gentleness with each other daily.

Day 21: Revival in Marriage

"Will You not revive us again, that Your people may rejoice in You?" Psalm 85:6

Prayer: Lord, refresh and revive our love. Renew the joy and passion of our marriage.

Day 22: Protection from the Enemy

"No weapon formed against you shall prosper,
And every tongue which rises against you in judgment
You shall condemn. This is the heritage of the servants of the Lord,
And their righteousness is from Me,"
Says the Lord." Isaiah 54:17

Prayer: Father, protect our marriage from every attack of the enemy. Surround us with Your peace.

Day 23: Contentment

"Godliness with contentment is great gain." 1 Timothy 6:6

Prayer: Lord, help us be content in every season, trusting in Your great provision.

Day 24: Communication

"Let your speech always be with grace, seasoned with salt, that you may know how you ought to answer each one." Colossians 4:6

Prayer: Father, teach us to speak with kindness, listen with patience, and understand each other.

Day 25: Healing from Hurts

"He heals the brokenhearted and binds up their wounds." Psalm 147:3

Prayer: Lord, heal every hidden hurt in our marriage. Restore us fully with Your love.

Day 26: Hospitality

"Do not forget to entertain strangers, for by so doing some have unwittingly entertained angels." Hebrews 13:2

Prayer: Father, make our home a place of welcome and blessing for others.

Day 27: Fruitfulness

"By this My Father is glorified, that you bear much fruit." John 15:8

Prayer: Lord, make our marriage fruitful in love, service, and spiritual growth.

Day 28: Perseverance

"And let us not grow weary while doing good…" Galatians 6:9

Prayer: Father, give us perseverance to keep doing good to people, loving, serving, and trusting You together.

Day 29: Legacy of Faith

"One generation shall praise Your works to another..." Psalm 145:4

Prayer: Lord, let our marriage give a legacy of faith for our children and generations to come.

Day 30: Good Perspective

"Two are better than one... for if either of them falls, one can help the other up." Ecclesiastes 4:9–10

Prayer: Lord, give us a loving and healthy perspective in our marriage. Help us see each other with grace, patience, and understanding. Strengthen our unity and teach us to build each other up every day.

Day 31: Thanksgiving for Marriage

"Oh, give thanks to the Lord, for He is good! For His mercy endures forever." Psalm 136:1

Prayer: Lord, thank You for the gift of our marriage. May we always honor You with our love and commitment. In Jesus' Mighty Name, Amen.

This 31-day prayer journey is just the beginning. Praying together daily builds a habit of *spiritual intimacy, unity, and strength.* As couples continue beyond these 31 days, their marriage will increasingly reflect the love of Christ and shine as a light to others.

(B)
Couple's Discussion Questions

"Counsel in the heart of man is like deep water, But a man of understanding will draw it out." Proverbs 20:5

I remember when my husband and I were newly in love. I would often tell him, "I have a question," and as a Dutch man, he would simply look in my eyes and reply, "Yeah," meaning he had no idea what I wanted to ask. And to be honest, I didn't know either! I just knew I had a question, even though I couldn't explain it. Many couples experience this: wanting to talk, wanting to connect, but not knowing how to begin.

This chapter will help you in this area, giving you direction, clarity, and guidance in asking meaningful questions that strengthen your marriage covenant.

Healthy marriages thrive on *intentional communication*. But many couples either avoid deep conversations or only talk about surface issues. This appendix provides fifty guided questions to help you and your spouse connect emotionally, spiritually, and practically.

Set aside time each week, perhaps a *"Marriage Conversation Night"* to go through a few questions. Remember: listen with love, don't rush, and always end with prayer.

1. Communication and Connection

1. What is one thing I do that makes you feel most loved?

2. When was the last time you felt truly heard by me? How can I listen better?

3. How can we improve the way we talk during disagreements?

4. Do you feel safe sharing your struggles with me? Why or why not?

5. What is one small habit we can add to make our daily conversations more meaningful?

Reflection: James 1:19 says, *"Let every man be swift to hear, slow to speak, slow to wrath."*

2. Love, Romance, and Intimacy

6. What does romance mean to you personally?

7. How can we be more intentional about physical affection?

8. Are there ways I can better meet your emotional or physical needs?

9. What was your favorite date we ever had, and why?

10. How can we bring more fun and laughter into our marriage?

Prayer Prompt: Lord, help us to keep the flame of love burning in our marriage.

3. Faith and Spiritual Growth

11. How do you see God working in our marriage right now?

12. What area of faith do you want to grow in this year?

13. How can I support your personal walk with God?

14. Are we praying enough together as a couple? How can we improve?

15. What Scripture has encouraged you recently, and why?

Reflection: Ecclesiastes 4:12 *"A threefold cord is not quickly broken."*

4. Conflict and Forgiveness

16. How do you usually feel when we argue?

17. Do you feel I forgive you quickly enough when mistakes happen?

18. What is the hardest thing for you when it comes to resolving conflict?

19. How can I show humility when we disagree?

20. What's one conflict from the past we handled well, and what can we learn from it?

Prayer Prompt: Lord, teach us to forgive as You forgave us (Ephesians 4:32).

5. Finances and Stewardship

21. How do you feel about our current financial state?

22. Are we in agreement about how money is spent in our home?

23. What financial goals should we set together for next year?

24. How can we be more generous as a couple?

25. Do you feel secure with the way we plan for the future?

Reflection: Proverbs 10:22 *"The blessing of the Lord makes one rich, and He adds no sorrow with it."*

This scripture encourages couples to see finances not as a source of stress, but as an area where God's blessing, wisdom, and unity can flow. When a husband and wife steward their resources together with purpose, generosity, and faith, they open the door for God's peace, provision, and supernatural increase in their home.

6. Dreams and Future Vision

26. What dreams or goals do you have that I may not fully know about?

27. Where do you see us in five years?

28. What extra good works do we want to do for our children or community?

29. Are we pursuing our God-given purpose together?

30. How can we take a step of faith toward a shared dream this year?

Prayer Prompt: Lord, align our dreams with Your plans for our lives.

7. Parenting and Family Life (if applicable)

31. How do you feel about the way we parent?

32. What's one thing we can do differently to bless our children?

33. How can we better show unity in front of them?

34. What spiritual values do we most want to teach them?

35. How do you want our children to describe our marriage when they are grown?

Reflection: Psalm 127:3 *"Behold, children are a heritage from the Lord, the fruit of the womb is a reward."*

8. Daily Life and Practical Support

36. What is one daily responsibility that feels overwhelming to you?

37. How can I better share the load at home?

38. What small act of kindness makes the biggest difference to you?

39. How can I be more intentional about showing appreciation?

40. Do you feel I notice your efforts enough?

9. Friendship and Fun

41. What activities bring us the most joy together?

42. If we had a free weekend with no responsibilities, how would you want to spend it?

43.   What's one hobby you'd like us to try together?

44.   Do you feel we play and laugh enough together?

45.   How can we nurture friendship at the core of our marriage?

Prayer Prompt: Lord, keep us best friends as well as life husband and wife.

10. Legacy and Growing Old Together

46.   What do you hope we will look back on with joy in 20 years?

47.   How do you want our love to inspire others?

48.   What does "growing old in God's love" mean to you?

49.   How can we keep serving God together in our old age?

50.   If we wrote a "marriage testimony," what would you want it to say?

Reflection: Psalm 92:14 *"They shall still bear fruit in old age; they shall be fresh and flourishing."*

How to Use These Questions

Weekly date night: Pick 3–4 questions to talk about over dinner.

Monthly check-in: Go through an entire category together.

Prayer tie-in: End each session by praying over what you shared.

Encouragement: Great marriages aren't built by chance; they are built by choice. These questions are not for criticizing each other but for *understanding, deepening, and celebrating* your covenant. As you talk, laugh, and sometimes even cry, you'll notice God weaving your hearts even closer together.

(C)
Scriptures for a Healthy Marriage

And above all these things put on love, which is
the bond of perfection." Colossians 3:14

The Word of God is the strongest foundation for a lasting marriage. Scriptures have the power to renew the mind, heal wounds, strengthen commitment, and remind couples of God's vision for their covenant. In this section, you'll find *carefully chosen Bible passages* to meditate on, pray with, and declare over your marriage.

You and your spouse can read them aloud together, memorize key verses, or even write them on cards to place around your home. Let these Scriptures become living seeds of faith in your hearts.

1. Scriptures on Love and Unity

1 Corinthians 13:4–7 *"Love suffers long and is kind; love does not envy; love does not parade itself, is not puffed up; does not behave rudely, does not seek its own, is not provoked, thinks no evil; does not rejoice in iniquity, but rejoices in the truth; bears all things, believes all things, hopes all things, endures all things."*

Reflection: Love is the heartbeat of marriage. Meditate on this passage and ask, "How can I love my spouse in action today?"

Colossians 3:14 *"But above all these things put on love, which is the bond of perfection."*

Prayer Prompt: Lord, help us to always put on love.

Amos 3:3 *"Can two walk together, unless they are agreed?"*

Reflection: Unity requires agreement. Are there areas in your marriage where you need to seek understanding and agreement?

2. Scriptures on Forgiveness and Grace

Ephesians 4:31–32 *"Let all bitterness, wrath, anger, clamor, and evil speaking be put away from you, with all malice. And be kind to one another, tenderhearted, forgiving one another, even as God in Christ forgave you."*

Reflection: Forgiveness is the oil that keeps the marriage wheel from seizing up. Without it, resentment builds walls.

Matthew 6:14–15 *"For if you forgive men their trespasses, your heavenly Father will also forgive you. But if you do not forgive men their trespasses, neither will your Father forgive your trespasses."*

Prayer Prompt: Lord, help us forgive quickly, remembering how much You have forgiven us.

3. Scriptures on Peace and Joy in the Home

Philippians 4:6–7 *"Be anxious for nothing, but in everything by prayer and supplication, with thanksgiving, let your requests be made known to God; and the peace of God, which surpasses all understanding, will guard your hearts and minds through Christ Jesus."*

Reflection: Worry robs marriages of peace. Bring your concerns together before God in prayer.

Psalm 16:11 *"You will show me the path of life; in Your presence is fullness of joy; at Your right hand are pleasures forevermore."*

Prayer Prompt: Lord, fill our home with Your presence and Your joy.

Romans 15:13 *"Now may the God of hope fill you with all joy and peace in believing, that you may abound in hope by the power of the Holy Spirit."*

Reflection: Hope, peace, and joy come from God's Spirit, not circumstances.

4. Scriptures on Unity and Purpose

Ecclesiastes 4:9-10 *"Two are better than one, because they have a good reward for their labor. For if they fall, one will lift up his companion…"*

Reflection: Marriage is a union. Ask each other: "How can I help lift you up this week?"

Genesis 2:18 *"And the Lord God said, 'It is not good that man should be alone; I will make him a helper comparable to him.'"*

Prayer Prompt: Lord, thank You for making us husband and wife in life and ministry.

Philippians 2:2 *"Fulfill my joy by being like-minded, having the same love, being of one accord, of one mind."*

Reflection: Marriage thrives when both pursue the same vision and values.

5. Scriptures on Faithfulness and Endurance

Malachi 2:14–15 *"Yet she is your companion and your wife by covenant. But did He not make them one, having a remnant of the Spirit? And why one? He seeks Godly offspring. Therefore take heed to your spirit, and let none deal treacherously with the wife of his youth."*

Reflection: God views marriage as a sacred covenant, not a temporary contract.

Hebrews 13:4 *"Marriage is honorable among all, and the bed undefiled; but fornicators and adulterers God will judge."*

Prayer Prompt: Lord, keep our hearts pure and our marriage bed undefiled.

James 1:12 *"Blessed is the man who endures temptation; for when he has been approved, he will receive the crown of life which the Lord has promised to those who love Him."*

How to Use These Scriptures Together

Daily Reading: Pick one passage to read together every evening.

Declaration: Speak them aloud as faith confessions (e.g., "Our marriage walks in love and unity").

Prayer: After reading, pray a short prayer applying the verse to your marriage.

Memorization: Each spouse memorizes one verse per week and shares what it means to them.

Journaling: Write reflections or answered prayers connected to these Scriptures in a joint journal.

Encouragement

God's Word is living and powerful (Hebrews 4:12). As you plant these Scriptures into your marriage, and many more Scriptures, including the book of *Song of Solomon*, expect fruit: greater unity, deeper love, peace that overcomes conflict, and joy that cannot be shaken.

Let your marriage be built not just on feelings or circumstances, but on the eternal foundation of God's Word.

(D)
Couple's Declarations
& Affirmations

As a couple, the words you speak carry power. Declarations rooted in God's Word build faith, restore unity, and create an atmosphere of peace in your home. Speak these affirmations daily together if possible.

1. Declarations of Unity

We are one flesh, united by God, and nothing will separate us. (Genesis 2:24; Matthew 19:6)

Our hearts are knit together in love, respect, and understanding.

We stand as one in life, purpose, and destiny.

The peace of God rules in our home and in our hearts. (Colossians 3:15)

2. Declarations of Love

We love each other with the love of Christ, unconditional, patient, and kind. (1 Corinthians 13:4–7)

We forgive quickly, speak kindly, and honor one another daily.

Our love grows stronger with every blessed day.

We are a testimony of God's love to the world.

3. Declarations of Faith & Prayer

We invite God into every decision, every plan, and every joy.

Our marriage is built on the Rock, Jesus Christ. (Matthew 7:24)

We are a praying couple, and through prayer, we always overcome.

The presence of God fills our home with joy, peace, and strength.

4. Declarations of Protection

No weapon formed against our marriage shall prosper. (Isaiah 54:17)

We reject every plan of the enemy against our unity and love.

Our children and household are covered by the blood of Jesus.

The Lord is our refuge, and He keeps us safe together. (Psalm 91:1–2)

5. Declarations of Blessing

Our marriage is fruitful, full of joy, and flourishing in every season.

We prosper in health, finances, and relationships, even as our souls prosper. (3 John 1:2)

Our home is a sanctuary of peace, happiness, and love.

We are blessed to be a blessing, and our marriage shines as a light in this world.

Daily Couple's Affirmation

"We declare that our marriage is a covenant blessed by God. We walk in love, unity, and purpose. We forgive, we honor, and we grow stronger together each day. Our home is filled with peace, joy, and the presence of God. We are one, and we shall always be together, by God's grace."

The Covenant Mindset

Marriage is a sacred calling, a divine gift, and a reflection of God's glory. As we conclude this book, it is my prayer that what you have read has not only enlightened your mind but also touched your heart. Marriage is more than a legal agreement, a romantic arrangement, or a lifestyle choice. It is a covenant; a holy promise made before God, a commitment that transcends circumstances, and a union that reflects heaven on earth.

Through this book, we have explored the foundations of a Godly marriage, the principles of unity, communication, forgiveness, intimacy, and spiritual alignment. We have seen that a marriage built on God's Word and prayer is not only sustainable but also fruitful, transformative, and victorious.

1. The Covenant Mindset

A recurring theme throughout this book is that marriage is a *covenant*, not a contract. Contracts are temporary, conditional, and limited by human expectations. Covenants, on the other hand, are *unconditional, eternal, and anchored in God's faithfulness.*

A covenantal marriage requires more than feelings or mutual convenience. It requires faith, commitment, and sacrifice. When you understand that your marriage is a covenant, you begin to act differently. You forgive more quickly, love more deeply, and persevere through challenges. You stop asking, "What's in it for me?" and start declaring, "How can I honor God and serve my spouse today?"

Living with a covenant mindset transforms your marriage from a relationship that depends on luck or circumstance into one that depends on God's grace, promises, and presence.

2. The Role of God in Marriage

Every principle discussed in this book points to one central truth: *God is the foundation of a strong marriage.* A marriage without God is like a house built on sand; it may appear sturdy at first, but it cannot withstand storms.

Prayer, shared worship, Bible study, and mutual spiritual growth are not optional extras; they are the lifeblood of a covenant marriage. When couples seek God together, they invite His wisdom, protection, and favor into their home. Ecclesiastes 4:12 says:

"A threefold cord is not quickly broken."

The threefold cord in marriage is the husband, the wife, and God. With God at the center, couples are empowered to navigate disagreements, endure hardships, and experience joy beyond what the world can offer. God does not just watch over marriages; He actively strengthens them.

3. Forgiveness, Grace, and Unity

The key to a lasting marriage is *forgiveness and grace.* Covenant love chooses to forgive even when it hurts, to extend grace even when it is undeserved, and to pursue unity all the time.

Forgiveness is not merely an act; it is a daily lifestyle. It involves releasing offense, letting go of past hurts, and refusing to allow resentment to take root. Couples who practice forgiveness create a fertile environment for love to flourish. Unity, on the other hand, is the commitment to align hearts, goals, and values. It is choosing togetherness over separation, compromise over stubbornness, and cooperation over pride.

A marriage rooted in forgiveness and unity becomes a sanctuary of peace, a haven where both spouses can grow emotionally, spiritually, and relationally.

4. Communication: Speaking Life and Listening with Love

Communication is one of the pillars of a successful marriage. Speaking with kindness, listening with patience, and resolving conflicts with humility are essential for sustaining love. Words are powerful; they can either build or destroy, encourage or wound, bless or not.

Couples must learn to speak life into each other daily. This involves verbal affirmations, declarations of faith, and expressions of love. Listening is equally important. Listening with empathy, without interrupting or judging, creates trust and intimacy.

Conflict can be transformational when handled biblically. Avoiding arguments and resolving disagreements with humility, respect, and prayerful wisdom.

5. Love in Action

Love is not just a feeling; it is a deliberate choice and consistent action. Throughout this book, we have emphasized practical ways to express love in marriage: serving one another, honoring each other, showing affection, maintaining romance, and prioritizing each other's well-being.

Intentional love nurtures intimacy and strengthens bonds. Small gestures of kindness, thoughtful words, and sacrificial actions demonstrate love more profoundly than grand declarations alone. Love in action ensures that your marriage is not only experienced by you but also witnessed by your children, family, and community.

6. Building a Home That Reflects Heaven

A Godly marriage extends beyond the couple. It creates a home that is a reflection of heaven; a place of peace, joy, prayer, and spiritual growth. When your home reflects God's Kingdom, it becomes a refuge for your family, a place of inspiration for friends, and a testament to the power of God's love.

Parents who model covenant love teach children to value faithfulness, respect, and service. The home becomes a training ground for Godly character, a sanctuary of safety, and a base for future generations to thrive.

7. Overcoming Challenges Together

Struggles can test the strongest couples. But covenant marriages are resilient because they face challenges together, with God's guidance. Trials become opportunities for growth. Couples who pray together, seek counsel together, and support each other emotionally and spiritually emerge stronger, more united, and more in love. Hardship reveals the depth of your commitment and strengthens your covenant bond.

8. Daily Habits for a Covenant Marriage

To experience the fullness of a covenant marriage, couples must develop intentional daily habits:

- *Daily prayer together*: Invite God into your decisions, conflicts, and celebrations.

- *Regular Bible study*: Build wisdom, understanding, and spiritual alignment.

- *Affirmations and declarations*: Speak life, blessing, and covenant promises over each other.

- *Acts of service:* Serve your spouse as Christ served the Church.

- *Quality time:* Prioritize relationship over busyness.

These habits transform marriage from ordinary to extraordinary. They create a rhythm of intimacy, faithfulness, and joy that sustains couples through every season.

9. The Eternal Perspective

Finally, a covenant marriage has an eternal perspective. Marriage is not only for earthly fulfillment; it is a spiritual assignment. It is a union in God's Kingdom, a platform to demonstrate Christ's love.

Couples who embrace this perspective understand that their union is more than personal happiness; it is a testimony to the world, a reflection of God's glory, and a foundation for generational blessings.

10. A Call to Commitment

As we close this book, I urge every couple to *recommit to the covenant of marriage.* Whether you are newly married or have been together for decades, it is never too late to realign your hearts with God and each other.

Commit to:

- Loving unconditionally

- Forgiving continually

- Praying faithfully

- Serving selflessly

- Growing spiritually together

When you do, your marriage becomes not only a personal blessing but also a *testimony*.

Walking in the beauty of Marriage

Marriage is a journey; a sacred adventure filled with joy, challenge, growth, and divine purpose. The principles in this book are not meant to be mere knowledge; they are meant to be *practiced daily*. As you live out covenant love, intentional communication, forgiveness, and spiritual unity, you will discover that your marriage can indeed be like heaven on earth.

Remember, a good marriage is not found; it is *built*. It is built through prayer, obedience, faithfulness, and the daily decision to love. It is built with God at the center, and it is sustained by grace.

Walk in the covenant today, walk in love every day, and watch as God transforms your marriage into a living testimony of His glory. Your marriage can be a heaven not just for you, but for everyone who witnesses it.

Blessing & Prayer for Couples

Heavenly Father, we thank You for the sacred gift of marriage. We honor You as the center of every home and the foundation of every union. Lord, we pray that You bless every couple who has read this book, committing their hearts, minds, and lives to You.

Father, we declare:

That every marriage is a covenant blessed by You.

That love, respect, and faithfulness flow abundantly in every relationship.

That every home is filled with peace, joy, and Your presence.

That forgiveness and grace reign over every misunderstanding and offense.

Lord, we pray for *unity and intimacy* in every marriage:

Strengthen husbands to love their wives sacrificially, just as Christ loves the Church.

Empower wives to honor and support their husbands in love and respect.

Unite couples together in a threefold cord, with You, Oh Lord, at the center.

Protect marriages from the schemes of the enemy, from division, bitterness, and discouragement.

We declare *blessings of provision and prosperity*:

Let every household flourish in health, peace, finances, and purpose.

May children grow in Godly character and experience the love of both parents.

May every couple fulfill the destiny You have ordained for them, walking in joy, favor, and divine alignment.

Father, we pray for *spiritual growth and guidance*:

Let couples walk daily in prayer, study of Your Word, and obedience to Your Spirit.

Teach them to communicate with grace, resolve conflicts with wisdom, and love unconditionally.

Grant them discernment to make decisions that honor You and strengthen their covenant.

We bless every couple with *heavenly love that endures*:

May their love reflect Your glory and inspire others.

May their home be a sanctuary of peace, a refuge of comfort, and a light to the world.

May they grow stronger together with each year, rooted in faith, hope, and love.

Lord, we thank You for the gift of covenant marriage. May every couple reading this be empowered to live in covenant, walking faithfully, serving joyfully, and loving deeply. Let their marriage be a testament to Your goodness and a reflection of Your heavenly design.

We seal this prayer in the mighty name of Jesus Christ, Amen.

Invitation

A marriage built in Christ is a marriage built on an unshakable foundation. Love becomes deeper, forgiveness flows more freely, and peace fills the home when Jesus is at the center. The marriage covenant is not only a promise between two people: *husband and wife*, but a sacred vow made before God; a covenant He delights to strengthen, sustain, and bless.

No matter where you are today in your journey, newly married, rebuilding, or seeking God's direction, the Lord desires to walk with you. He is the Author of love, the restorer of broken hearts, and the One who keeps every covenant for all generations. When Christ is honored in the home, the Holy Spirit fills the atmosphere with unity, joy, wisdom, and divine protection.

If you have not yet given your life to Jesus Christ, there is no greater decision you can ever make. He is inviting you today into His love, His forgiveness, and His eternal family. Salvation is not complicated; it is simply responding to the love of God, Who sent His Son to die for your sins and rise again so you may have life eternally.

If you desire to receive Jesus Christ as your Lord and Savior, you may pray from your heart:

"Lord Jesus, I come to You today. I confess that I am a sinner and I need Your mercy. I believe You died for me and rose again. I surrender my life to You. Forgive me, cleanse me, and make me Your child. I invite You into my heart and into my home. From today, I choose to follow You. Thank You for saving me. In Jesus' Precious name I pray. Amen."

If you prayed this prayer sincerely, you are now a child of God. I encourage you to join a Bible-believing church, grow in God's Word, and allow the Holy Spirit to guide your marriage and your life.

May the Lord bless your home, strengthen your covenant, and fill your life with His unending grace.

Jesus Christ remains the center today, tomorrow, and forever. Amen!

About the Author

Pastor Mariana is a devoted Bible teacher, an intercessor, and a passionate lover of God, with a deep desire to see lives transformed through the power of prayer and the Word of God. She serves with a deep commitment to nurturing believers, strengthening pastors, and building Christ-centered communities across nations. Her ministry carries a strong emphasis on revival, discipleship, and the restoration of families through the presence of the Holy Spirit.

She is the founder of Stichting Shekinah – Help the Needy in Maastricht, a foundation dedicated to supporting vulnerable families, empowering youth, and touching lives with the compassion of Christ. Her heart for missions has opened doors in Central Africa, Israel, and Europe, where she continues to teach, encourage, and equip the Body of Christ.

Mariana is the author of several impactful Christian books, including *The Creative Power of Prayer*, *How to Choose a Godly Spouse*, *70 Kinds of Prayers*, *A Happy Christian*, and *Teenagers' World*. Her writings focus on prayer, spiritual growth, the prophetic, and walking in the fullness of God's calling.

She is the host of BIBLE STUDY NETWORK, her YouTube Bible teaching ministry, where she helps believers understand Scripture chapter by chapter. She also leads online Bible studies and mentors young believers, inspiring them to live boldly for Christ.

Mariana is a wife, a mother, and a vessel of God's grace dedicated to seeing homes strengthened, destinies awakened, and nations touched by the Gospel.

Her life message is simple yet powerful:

"Prayer changes everything, because God changes everything."

To contact the author, please write to:
Miradorplein 39, 6222 TE Maastricht; The Netherlands
Or call: *+31 (0) 685 261 335*
E-mail: *info@shekinahevangelicalchurch.com*

Please feel free to share your testimony about how this book has helped you. You are also welcome to include your prayer requests.

Other Books by the Same Author

Notes